"This book is a MUST READ for anyone who is planning on getting married or has already taken the trip down the aisle!"
D.H. – Fargo, ND

"Like my Mother used to say,
"Forewarned is forearmed"."
R.L. – Chicago, IL

"After reading this book,
I'm thrilled that my wedding was so 'average'."
T.F. – Duluth, MN

"Absolutely hilarious!
This is the strategic, guerilla handbook
to planning a successful wedding."
E.S. – Minneapolis, MN

"This book is a page-turner! Once you pick it up, you won't be able to put it down until you're done!"
F.I. – Los Angeles, CA

"I Do"

15 Years
of
True Stories
from a
Wedding
Videographer

By Kiersten Hall

www.idovideostories.com

"I Do" 15 Years of True Stories
    from a Wedding Videographer
Title ID: 5509543
ISBN-13: 978-1512282283
www.idovideostories.com

This book is a work of non-fiction.
Full names have been withheld for privacy purposes.
The experiences, impressions and anecdotes
I relate remain substantially intact.

Between 1990 through 2006, I co-owned "I Do" Productions
Wedding Videography. As a co-owner, I worked with the
couples for both pre and post-nuptial, as well as videotaped
and edited the weddings. At the height of the successful
years, "I Do" actually had three video crews going out on
Saturdays. The stories within this book are of the couples
and weddings I personally worked with, including videotaped
and/or edited.

"I Do"

15 Years
of
True Stories
from a
Wedding
Videographer

Judy & Nels —
Cheers &
Enjoy! :)

A special thank you
to all the people who ever said to me,
"I bet you have a lot of stories."
Well, everyone was correct.
'I Do' have a lot of stories,
and here they are...

Videography:
The art of recording images with a video camera.
Correct pronunciation: vid-ee-ah-graf-ee

Videographer:
The person who uses the video camera to record images.
Correct pronunciation: vid-ee-ah-graf-er

Wedding Videographer:
Someone who wants to be self-employed and, at the same time, share in others' joy. (True translation: Someone who works every weekend at the cost of missing their own family's special events and, at the same time, agonize that something will go wrong during a once-in-a-lifetime event and will be held accountable.)

Take it from the Top

"Once upon a time, in a land far, far away…"

Isn't that the way a book of fairytales should begin? Okay, actually this particular story began in the late 1980s while my fiancé and I were in college. As an elective, my fiancé had taken a photography course which eventually led to applying for, and accepting a position with a local wedding photographer, as a 'go-fer', at $40 per Saturday. He spent his weekends setting up photography equipment, tripods, helping set up the shots, straightening veils and trains, loading film into cameras, keeping little children happy during the photography prior to the ceremony, and in a timely manner, making sure the car was driven up to the church steps and the reception doors to pick up the photographer. Since the summer of 1987, my Saturday night dates, with my fiancé, started at 1:00am when he would get home and then proceed to tell me about the wedding he attended as well as the different shots and trade secrets he learned during that day's wedding.

In 1989, this photographer decided to add 'videography' to his wedding photography packages. My fiancé, possessing an innate talent for electronics, quickly was assigned to the videography end of the photographer's business.

In the meantime, I had completed my college degree and was busy establishing a career for myself, and my Saturday night dates continued starting at 1:00am filled with talk of camera angles, equipment failures and repairs, and more trade secrets and good ideas. Although I had never dreamed of being a videographer, myself, I was subconsciously taking notes for my future career...

In 1990, when it came time for my personal fairytale wedding (I say 'fairytale' sarcastically - more on this later), two of the most important details included the photography and the videography. Our wedding would only happen once and we wanted to preserve the day in its entirety so, not only could we enjoy reliving it over the years, but could also pass it onto our children and grandchildren. Unfortunately, along with being naïve (this was, after all, the first and only wedding we had ever planned), we were also in a rather awkward position. First of all, my other half was working every weekend so, since this photographer was booked solid, he *must* be good. We had no idea there were other photography styles out there, in the big world, and we surely couldn't have hired a different photographer/videographer to do our wedding because that would be rude. We couldn't *not* invite this person – that would be rude, too. So, we told him about our plans with hopeful expectations that we would receive some sort of a deal... A discount, especially since our wedding was on a Friday evening. Nope, no deal... Not even an itty-bitty, teensy-weensy deal. Full price all the way - typical of our luck. So, we were stuck; the weekend employer was our photographer/videographer, for our upcoming nuptials.

Though there are many artistic styles available, our photographs are all of the 'smile-and-say-cheese' variety; boring. If only I knew then, what I know now...

But the video would be better, right? Video captures all the sights and sounds of the day, not just a click in time... Our video was pathetic. It never occurred to us to ask that since the regular videographer was now on the altar getting married, himself, who would be in the balcony operating the video camera? Not a soul, that's who... Although we had paid full price, the video camera did not come with an operator. The camera's view was centered on the altar and was stationary. Our processional is not on tape. Everyone who walked up to the altar just suddenly appeared at the bottom of the screen when they entered the camera's eye. When we lit our unity candle, which was placed off to the side, we momentarily walked off the screen, and then walked back on. There were no close-ups. No camera followed us when we stepped off the altar steps to give roses to our Moms; nothing. The audio left much to be desired, too. The ambient microphone on the camera picked up the whirring of the ceiling fans, and just a faint hint of our readings. When the Pastor spoke, his voice was full of echo. Ideally, with the wireless microphone my groom wore on his lapel, we should have had our vows recorded, clean and crisp. We didn't get those, either. The professional photographer, *we had to have,* didn't bother to replace the 9-volt batteries in the wireless microphone's transmitter and receiver. Yes, for an extra $4.95, we could have had our vows on tape. And at the end, after the kiss viewed from 150 feet away, we (predictably) walked off the bottom of the screen. So, armed with the experience of planning our own wedding along with our dismay at the photographer whom we felt compelled to hire for simple still photos and a pathetic $1,200 videotape of our wedding, we embarked on our own business: "I Do" Productions. Looking back now, we should have taken more time to think things through and we should have picked up on what we had learned from our own wedding before we jumped into this new adventure. However, if "I Do" Productions had not been started in 1990, I would have no stories to tell. No book to write. And what fun would that be?

All the stories in this collection of memories are true whether they are funny, sad, far-fetched, have sarcastic undertones, or stop and make you think. I have enjoyed remembering the past and sharing these stories. At times during writing, my children and I have been downright laughing and at other times we have found ourselves hoping that these past clients are doing better. I have estimated, over the years, I have personally come in contact with over 250,000 people through "I Do" which has given me a lot of stories to tell. Each wedding that I have ever done provides at least one story. With this book, I have compiled my personal memories that have stood out over 15 years of being in the wedding videography business and I have done my best to convey these tales to you. Of course, the best way to have experienced these stories was to be there, but I hope you will enjoy reading this book as much as I have enjoyed writing it.

My Wedding Memories

As I mentioned in the preceding chapter, I should have taken into account what I had learned while I was planning my own 'fairytale' wedding.

Along with the mishaps of our photography and videography, we had trouble securing a church and a reception hall for the same day. I had become so exasperated with suggestions from people! "Have your ceremony on one day and then two weeks later, have your reception." Yeah, that makes a lot of sense.

Why hadn't I thought of that myself? Hmmm. (This suggestion, of course, was made by someone trying to book their reception hall.) I was a hair away from planning my wedding for any Friday that would fall on the 13th! I knew that with a date like that, I wouldn't have much competition in reserving both a church and a reception hall for the same day!!! No worries, though; I lucked out with Friday, July 27th. I should have taken this as my very first hint that I should have run the opposite way – from the wedding industry. Apparently, I'm either thick, or a glutton for punishment, or both.

Now, let's see. What other 'challenges' presented themselves regarding our wedding? You know, the 'challenges' we should have taken into account before we leapt with both feet into the deep end of the wedding videography industry...

Well, my Mom was completely against the video (you can laugh), the ice sculpture and the horse and carriage; all of which came out of my own pocket. I wanted only two bridesmaids; a Matron and a Maid of Honor. Neither of these two people were my sister or my future sister-in-law. I was told that I must have my sister and my future sister-in-law included in my bridal party and in turn, when their weddings came around, I would be included in their bridal parties. Both are now married and so much for promises; I was not included in either one of my sister-in-law's *two* weddings, and my very own sister even went so far as to tell me that myself and my family were under strict orders to stay away from her wedding locations and that we were absolutely not invited... If we showed up, the police would be called and charges filed. Geez! So much for family politics and doing the 'right thing...'

After I agreed to have two additional bridesmaids, my sister-in-law-to-be was unwilling to get her shoes dyed in the same batch as the other bridesmaid's shoes. For $1.00 more, she could have had shoes that were the same shade. I even offered to pay the $1.00 difference, but no. I guess that was too much to ask. My mother-in-law-to-be also insisted that she would hem the dress for my sister-in-law. Again, I offered to pay for the alterations, but no go. It's funny to look at the pictures with all of us standing on the altar, in a row. All the dresses are fairly equal in the length except for my sister-in-law's dress and her off-color shoes.

Our church wedding coordinators decided, with their infinite wisdom, that since it was so hot and humid, they would turn off the few 100-watt lights which somewhat, illuminated the altar are to keep it cooler in the sanctuary (it didn't help.) I wasn't even aware that they had made this decision and after I looked at the video, I wish they had kept their infinite wisdom to themselves. Not only did they take away the only source of 'subject' light, but because the entire front of the church is lit up permanently with natural window light and hidden lighting fixtures, any subject against a brightly lit background was going to be dark. Regarding our wedding video, along with turning on the video camera (thankfully our photographer remembered to at least do this), he also opened up the iris on the camera to allow more light to enter the camera in an effort to brighten up the subjects (us) in an already dark situation. When this is done, the picture becomes extremely grainy in very dark situations, and if you don't bother to zoom in close on your subject, well, it's just pointless. Since my groom had always done the videography for this guy, when it came to our wedding day you could tell that this photographer was unfamiliar with a video camera, nor did he know what he was supposed to do when shooting this type of event. By the way, the temperature outside was 98 degrees and there was an approaching thunderstorm. To cap it off (but you probably already guessed), there was no air-conditioning in the church.

The flowers that were delivered were not what I ordered. That would explain why the florist literally came into the church, dropped the box of flowers on the floor and left abruptly. I had paid for 11 calla lilies to be part of an arm-spray which included ivy with a variety of grasses, and would cascade down toward the floor. Instead, I received 11 calla lilies with three foot stems which looked like they were pulled out of a garden that morning; they were loosely held together with a 1/4" inch wide, grosgrain ribbon. Fortunately, my Mom had brought some sandwiches for the attendants to eat before the service (no fainting allowed!) and used the plastic wrap and a rubber band to bundle up the loose ends of the stems (complete with leaking chlorophyll.) To include something 'old,' I had a bow from my Grandmother's wedding bouquet and fortunately, it covered up the mess. As long as I held the 'bouquet' just right, no one knew. (I did get a 50% refund afterwards.)

Hmmm, the next issue. Our photographer continued to reprimand our family and guests about taking pictures – he wanted to ensure he got reprint orders (we were so happy we invited and hired him!)

The next mishap would have to be while my Matron of Honor, Best Man, my new husband, and I were in the horse and carriage we had chosen as a special touch for the ride to our reception; we took a left turn into the parking lot of our reception hall and all of the water which had pooled on the vinyl roof of the carriage (remember the impending storm?) poured into the carriage and onto my dress and the envelope which held our signed marriage license. Once we got to the front door of the reception, and we were getting out of the carriage, my *now* mother-in-law blocked my way and asked why no one else got to ride in the carriage? Before she would move out of my way, I had to explain to her that there was only room for four people (in the four-person carriage) and that if she had her heart set on a ride, the carriage company would be at the reception site for the remainder of the hour.

But, continuing, a handful of family members bickered about why their friends couldn't sit at the reserved parent and grandparent tables. Let's not forget our DJ who wouldn't start the music until he was paid an additional $35 in cash for bringing larger speakers (which we recommended that he do.) Since he would only accept cash, we wound up having one of our groomsmen take our cash card and drive to an ATM to get cash during the dinner. Once the dance was to begin, the DJ started it off by saying, "We are here to celebrate with... Umm, a wedding reception for..." He forgot our names! He was busy fumbling around with papers in front of him trying to find our names! One of our guests sitting next to the dance floor repeatedly whispered our names and finally, after four whispering attempts, the DJ stuttered out, "We're here for Kristin and John!" By the way, my name is 'Kiersten', which is pronounced completely different from 'Kristin.' To top off my already mounting suspicions that my DJ was a complete moron, he played the wrong first song. After all these years, this mistake still irks me. After the reception finished, he admitted to us that the speakers had been 'red lining' all night and he was glad that we suggested bringing larger speakers. Professional DJ? I think not.

Now, sane people would say to themselves, "That particular wedding and all of its 'challenges' is all one couple would ever need." Not us. We figured if we lived through that wedding, we could get through any wedding. We also knew that we could do a better job with videography than what we had from our wedding. So, "I Do" Productions began in 1990 on a shoestring budget, a dream, and some certainty that I could be trained to run a camera, too.

Relative Reasoning(s)
We had a *very supportive* family...

❤ In response to the start of my new business, my Mom told me to cut my hair, learn how to type, and get a real job.

❤ My husband's grandmother said we would be lucky to do a few dozen weddings and the business would go nowhere.

❤ When it came to my sister's wedding 11 years later, I offered to video tape her wedding day for free, and she informed me that she thought video was not important and pointless. Then she threatened to have us arrested if we showed up at her wedding ceremony and/or reception.

❤ When my sister-in-law's wedding rolled around, the two of us and our daughter were finding our spots around the reserved family tables when someone on the catering staff noted we were using cameras. She immediately halted our activity and demanded that the 'help' must sit back by the kitchen. We gently explained to her that although we were the videographers, we were also family members, and would be able to get a much better shot of the bride and groom from the family tables. Then she gently explained to us that although we were family, at the bride's request, we were to sit in the back by the kitchen. The buffet table ended about ten feet from where we were assigned to sit, and all of the relatives who went through the buffet line would stop at our table and ask us, "What in the world are you guys doing sitting back here?" And say, "You should be up at the family tables."

Ain't family grand? ♡

Prospective Customers

Okay, the paperwork is done and I'm starting the new business. But who are my prospective customers? Where do I find them? How about a bridal show? Inevitably, at every bridal show I have ever done, there will be at least one person if not more who will come up to my booth and ask, "What do you do?" This person is standing in front of a booth with three televisions placed on a raised table immediately below a large vinyl banner that reads:

"I Do" Productions
Wedding Videography

Oh, how many times I was tempted to answer, "I make wedding cakes and drive the limo." I know these people are overwhelmed when they come to bridal shows, but they really should observe before they ask this question. Actually, believe it or not, some people even go as far as to pick up one of our brochures and look through it and/or momentarily will watch one of our wedding videos on the TV screen and still ask that question. "So, what do you do?" is by far the funniest question I have been asked at shows.

I also get young ladies who bring their already-married friends or relatives with them to the show. The bride-to-be stops at my booth and her entourage excitedly works to convince her that she "should definitely hire someone to do a video!" They will go on about how they didn't get a video, how they thought it was unimportant, how they should have reserved a videographer, and finally that if they could do it over, they would definitely get a videographer. I have often thought of hiring these people to stand in front of my booth and tell passers-by why they think videography is such a good idea. I wonder if they would take me up on that offer?

I have also had people from the extreme opposite end of that spectrum; the people who are just plain rude. I've had moms and their daughters come up to my booth and exclaim from the top of their lungs that they think videography is "stupid and a waste of money." Some will even pick up a brochure and when I tell them what I do (these are typically the people who ask that funny question), they toss the unfolded brochure back onto the table and walk away with a snort. Quite frankly, with attitudes like those, it's just as well they walk away although I really would have liked to have educated them about videography and explain how it is not a waste of money. They would have probably come to understand that people are more apt to sit down and watch a DVD of their wedding day than look through the still photographs. Their loss...

Open For Business

I'm in business! I'm back from the bridal show, and I have a list of all the brides who attended... Now I have to contact all of them. The first thing I'm going to do is mail out brochures and although I'm going to rack up a heck of a bill at the Post Office, there is no way I'm going to do cold-calling. I'm too chicken! What if someone said, "No?!?!?"

Every so often, after mailing a batch of brochures, I will receive a phone call from a bride who is a bit confused. I generally send brochures out with an offer of a 10% discount providing the couple reserves with us within 30 days (I will write that particular date on the brochure.) Most people, I think, get this. However, there are some who don't. At least a couple of times a year, I will get a call from a bride who will ask if I can extend this offer until her wedding date and then she will back up her question by explaining that her planned marriage does not fall within the prescribed 30-day period of the offer. Rather than falling off my chair in fits of hysterical laughter and consequently dropping the phone, I patiently point out she doesn't need to have her wedding before the expiration date; she just needs to reserve her wedding with us prior to the 30-day expiration of the offer. She can have her wedding on whatever day she chooses. Typically, when that situation is cleared up, the couple will reserve with me.

There was one other odd phone call pertaining to the 10% offer on a brochure. One bride was so excited to talk with me, she was just giddy. She asked about the different services and options that were offered with the videography packages. She was telling me all about her wedding and when and where it was. She said she didn't need an appointment to see my work. She just wanted to draw up a contract, right then and there, over the phone. That was a great phone call – until I asked, "How did you hear of "I Do" Productions?" She had told me that she had just received my brochure in the mail that offered 100% off any video package. I asked her if she was sure about the 100% since I was fairly certain it was a 10% discount. She assured me it definitely said 100% and I could hear she was shuffling her papers to prove me wrong. After a few seconds, the sound of thrashing papers stopped, and she exclaimed, "Never mind! I'm not interested in video!" and quickly hung up.

Sometimes, couples would need to leave messages on my voicemail and there would be specific instances that made me question both the business and the people who called. First were those who would call, multiple times on a Saturday, leaving messages to call them back immediately and/or that they would like to meet with me on that day. By the second or third "I Do" message, I would start to pick up on the frustration and anger in their voices. These people were calling on a Saturday! Hmmm, let me think really hard... What does "I Do" Productions Wedding Videography do on Saturdays??? Let me think... Oh!!! I know!!!! The owners of "I Do" Productions would not be in the office on Saturdays... They are out SHOOTING WEDDINGS ON SATURDAYS!!! They would leave messages such as, "What kind of operation is this?", "You aren't very professional!", "I demand a phone call today!", "I've left three messages so far, and if someone doesn't call me back soon, I'm not hiring you!" When I did get a chance to call them back the next day, I'd politely lead them through the question and answer game of "Let's remember what day it was yesterday and what do the owners of "I Do" Productions do every Saturday?" (They would usually apologize for their short fuses.)

Another message which would be left on my voicemail would be similar to this: "Hi, I'm getting married next September in the Twin Cities area and I have some questions about your videography services. I have been referred to you by one of my co-workers who used you for her wedding. Could you call me as soon as you get the chance? I'm looking forward to hearing from you soon.

Thanks." That's it! Okay, let's see if anything important is missing... Anything? Perhaps the pertinent information?

When these people call back and either talk with me directly, or leave another message, they start in with the "...I called a few days ago and I requested a return phone call from you. I was under the impression, from my co-worker, that you were a professional company." When I finally talked with them, I would remind them that they had neither left their name, phone number, co-worker's name, ceremony location, nor wedding date; nothing to go on so I couldn't return their message. After explaining why I had not called them back, and their blood pressure was returning to normal, they would typically respond with an "Oh, oops!"

When I used to hold appointments in my home, it was both good and bad. Good, since I had people coming over which meant I had to keep the house clean. The bad parts came in the form of 'no shows,' people expecting to eat and people standing on my furniture. Yes, standing on my furniture.

'No shows,' fortunately, were not the standard for appointments. But they did happen even after I would confirm the appointment with the couple. As for those who did show up for their appointments, most were just fine. However, there were a few who would ask about food. When I told them that potential clients just view a demo video and I answer any questions they may have, they would tell me, "At our catering appointment, we were able to sample foods." Or, "At the cake appointment, we were served cake and champagne." Once again, how I would have loved to have said, "Well, yes, you would get cake at your cake appointment and food samples at your catering appointment. Now you are getting video at your video appointment." But I never said that. Instead, I would just offer them what I had in the fridge or some Oreos from the cupboards, and they would just wind up dropping the subject altogether. As I recall, I don't believe those couples wound up booking with us. C'est la vie!

As for the furniture thing, some people get rather comfy when they watch TV. I had people putting their feet up on my coffee table - shoes on or off, didn't matter. The one person, who stood on my couch, was on a quest to terminate the life of a mosquito. With his shoe in his hand, he succeeded in fully squashing the offending insect and leaving the living room wall marked with the heel of his shoe and the disseminated body of the bug.

Speaking of 'creatures,' when "I Do" Productions first opened up for business, we had a 55-gallon salt water tank in the office, whose occupant's name was 'Ollie.' Ollie was an octopus from the Caribbean ocean, who unbeknownst to him, lived in Minnesota. For all the grooms and other members of the bridal entourages who came through our office (and who never really wanted to go to all of the endless appointments in the first place), they got to watch Ollie hunt his prey, and eat dinner. After bridal shows, Ollie ate well with the number of people we had over for appointments! Our pitch could have been: "I Do" Productions Wedding Videography (where goldfish meet their demise!) Or maybe not...

Regarding contracts, there are two that really stand out. The first is a wedding that originally contracted with me for a one-camera ceremony only. Two months later, they called and changed it to a two-camera event. Less than a month later, they called and added more hours of coverage to the package which would have had me at their event, almost up to the end of the reception; they would have had a lot of great footage – practically the entire day. However, four days before the wedding, the mother of the bride was on the phone with me again to take the video package back down to the one-camera ceremony only. I could hear the unhappiness in her voice and I could hear her husband, the father of the bride, in the room with her asking questions such as, "Do you really think a video is necessary?", "Do the video people really have to be there?", "Have we paid them anything yet?", "Can we cancel them?", and "Will they refund our money?" (You just get such a warm, fuzzy feeling when you know you are wanted at a wedding.)

I knew the mother of the bride was being put in an awkward position and I was completely sympathetic, so I told her it was no problem and not to worry. I would do the wedding itself and a relative could videotape at the reception so the toasts, candid pictures, and the first dance, etc. would be preserved on tape. I also recommended that this person should remember to use a tripod, bring a camera battery charger and that it would be a good idea to rent a wireless lapel microphone for a better direct audio feed during the toasts. She thanked me for the suggestions and ended the phone call by telling me that her husband didn't like the chairs at the country club, where the reception was being held, so they were going to rent chair slipcovers at the cost of $750.00. The father of the bride thought it was more important to be concerned about what the chairs at the reception looked like rather than preserving the once-in-a-lifetime memories of his daughter's special day.

Well, the wedding day came and went and when the video was ready to be delivered a month later, I called the mother of the bride to let her know that I would be mailing the tape. I asked her if the wedding went well and if the designated relative did a good job with the reception video. She confided in me that the wedding day was beautiful, but the relative had not brought a battery charger. Turned out that the reception video consisted of people standing around during the cocktail hour, in the dark... And people taking their seats for dinner, in the dark... The first person to stand and give a toast was the bride's sister, the Matron of Honor. The camera battery died around the sixth or seventh word of her toast and this relative had not brought extra batteries. So, that was the end of the video. Sadly, starting the night of the reception, the bride did not speak to her father. And as of this conversation, silence was still the rule. On a side note, thank goodness those chairs looked good!

The other contract that comes to mind is from a couple of years ago. Actually, on the surface, everything about this contract was just fine, nothing different. The couple had reserved my videography services ten months before their wedding date. Around five weeks prior to their date, the bride called me and told me, rather matter-of-factly, that the wedding was off. Four days later, she called me again to tell me that the wedding was back on. I told her that was wonderful, and I would also send out a new contract to her because I had already made cancellation notes on the original contract and filed it away. The next day, I transferred all the information from the original contract to the new one and mailed it out to her. A week later, the newly signed contract came back and the only thing that had been penned in and initialed was the groom's name; it had been crossed out and a new groom's name written in. A new groom four weeks prior to the wedding date! What is up with that? I really wanted to ask, but what question do you ask?! "So, are you upgrading before you sign on the dotted line?"

"I Do"

The wedding date arrived and no one hinted at the difference – no mention was made. The new groom's side had an equal number of guests as the bride's side. It was just a normal wedding like every other normal wedding – but it wasn't. These are the things that make   you   say,   "Hmmmm….."

What Can I Get For Under $500?

Eighty percent of the people who call me for information, from the start to the end of the conversation, are polite and tactful whether or not they hear what they want to hear regarding prices, packages, etc. However, there is the other twenty percent who are not. Most of these impolite and tacky conversations start with one of two statements:

"I've already spent thousands on my photographer and I don't want to spend any more than $500 on the video."

OR

"I didn't/don't want a video, but I've got a little left in my budget. What can I get for under $500?"

Might these be the same people who are most concerned about the slipcovers on their reception chairs? Once again, there are just some people you can't educate.

In a classic situation, a number of years ago, I received a phone call from a vice president of a bank who was making telephone calls for his daughter's upcoming wedding. He told me he was referred to me by their photographer whom I knew as reputable and rather expensive, I answered all of his questions and told him all about my packages and prices. I then asked him if he had any questions and he said, "Can't I get the entire day videotaped for like, $75?" I said, "No." And that was pretty much the end of our conversation.

Think. A vice president of a bank wants my video company to come out and shoot his daughter's entire wedding for $75! Let's talk in a language a banker might understand: Money. If there are four Saturdays in a month, and I only charge $75 per wedding, I will make a whopping (hold onto your bootstraps, Folks!!!) $300.00 per month! Whooppeee!!!!! People who flip burgers and ask if you'd like fries with your sandwich make more than $300 per month! The most this person is willing to splurge on his daughter's wedding video is only $75.00? Did he truly believe a person could support themselves, let alone an entire family, on $300 per month?

Does this person live in the real world? How did this person become a banker? I felt bad for his daughter.

Dear Mother-In-Law-To-Be...

These are fairly close to being exact copies of letters that would have been written by a couple of grooms for whom I actually shot videos:

Letter #1:

Dear Mother-In-Law-To-Be,

Last weekend, a few of us went boating and we had a great time. When we got back home, I was carrying the cooler off the boat and because I couldn't see where I was going, I miss-stepped and had an accident. Instead of stepping onto the dock, I stepped into the space between the dock and the boat and now my leg, a few of my ribs, and my arm are broken.

Fortunately, the wedding is still two weeks away and I will do my best to get better. I'm going to have to do something different for the tuxedo though because I don't think the casts are going to fit through the sleeve and the pant leg. I apologize in advance for the pictures. Maybe people can stand in front of me for the group shots so all of my casts can't be seen. Oh! One more thing before I forget: No one can hug me that day because of my broken ribs. Don't worry, everything will be fine.

Thanks,   Your Future Son-In-Law

Letter #2:

Dear Mother-In-Law-To-Be...

I am writing to you from the local hospital. At the moment, my head hurts too much to be able to tell you which hospital. Actually, it's probably good that I can't tell you the name because if I did, you'd come over and finish me off based on what I am about to tell you.

Yesterday afternoon at my bachelor party, I guess we all had a bit too much to drink. The best man was driving the golf cart and I thought it would be fun to sit out on the front of the golf cart, and that's when he ran it into a tree. I jumped off before the impact but didn't get out of the way in time and became pinned between the cart and the tree.

I know this is not what you want to hear six days before the wedding and if it makes you happy, I'm in a lot of pain. The doctors say I won't be out of here for at least a month, or maybe two. I know you've spent a lot of time planning the wedding and you've done a really nice job, but could you reschedule the wedding and call all the relatives, guests, and the people we have hired? Please don't be too mad.

Thanks,
Your Future Son-In-Law???

Where's My Church?

This topic just brings on a major headache. I'm personally amazed I didn't have a coronary, been diagnosed with an anxiety-induced illness, or been committed to a mental institution because of the stories you are about to read.

The basics for planning a wedding involves finding a particular place to hold your ceremony on a particular date at a particular time and then sharing this valuable information with everyone INCLUDING the businesses you hired for your day. While "I Do" Productions was in business, over the course of 16 years, we never missed a ceremony and/or reception. We had fulfilled every contract ever signed. But how the business had been so fortunate, in some cases, I don't know.

The first problems are those people who either work at the church, or the clergy who live in the rectory. These people apparently have never left the church, and had to return. If they did have to leave, they would, to this day, still be wandering around without a clue as to where they needed to get back to... Over the years, I had some interesting directions given to me which have sent me on wild goose chases!!! These people sound so kind and knowledgeable on the phone. (Surely they don't give wrong directions on purpose to wreak havoc in the lives of people who are supposed to be at the ceremony site at a particular time!)

I always leave about two to three hours of 'fudge' time prior to when I am contracted to be at an event. This practice has saved me on all of these little stories I am sharing with you here. I should also share with you that I always go by what is on the contract. It has all of my notes, the times, the locations, etc. The contract is what I live by! With this in mind...

Back in the late '90s, I had one wedding coming up which had two wedding coordinators working on it – same company, but partners. I had worked with both coordinators, numerous times, but only one at a time; they were both working on this wedding. As I have done with every couple over the past 15 years, I called the couple a week or so in advance of their wedding date, to confirm all necessary points and to see if there are any changes, questions, concerns, etc. In this case, however, the two wedding coordinators were the contacts for this wedding, not the bride or groom. The one coordinator whom I had dealt with most often was going to be out of town until two days before the wedding so, I called the one coordinator who was still in town. I went over the contract and all the pertinent points including the start times. Since the origination of the contract, the start time for this wedding was 6:30pm which meant that I would need to arrive at the church at 5:00pm to find a place to park, get a two-camera ceremony set up and finally, to look like I had calmly been prepared and hadn't been sweating when the guests started to arrive at 6:00pm (I was eight months pregnant.) I went over all of this information with the wedding coordinator and she confirmed with me the ceremony start time was set for 6:30pm.

There is no reason other than that by the grace of the heaven's above, before I left the house, I checked the invitation envelope for a map to the church since the coordinator I spoke with couldn't remember the directions, address, or cross-streets for the church. There wasn't a map so, I grabbed the entire invitation and figured that from the address printed on the invitation alone, I could find the church in this city. If I had trouble, I would stop at a gas station and ask for directions or look it up in the local phone book.

By 4:15pm, I had just dropped my two older children off at daycare and got into line at a fast food restaurant to pick up something to tide me over until dinner which would probably be served around 9:00pm. I was still 30 minutes away from the church, but had 45 minutes to get there. No problem. While sitting in line waiting for my food, I opened the invitation to look at the address of the church to see if I had any clue as to where it was or if I was going to have to stop and ask for directions as soon as I got into town. To my horror, not only did the invitation not have an address printed on it, but the ceremony time was listed as 5:30pm!!! (Just writing about this memory has elevated my blood pressure!) Needless to say, I did not wait for my food, but instead tore out of line and screeched out of the parking lot and onto the highway as fast I could. To just make things worse, this wedding took place on a Friday.

So, not only was I now running one hour late, but I had to put up with the beginning of rush hour traffic on a major trunk highway leading out of the city. I had 30 miles to go. I'm sweating. I'm stressed and the last time I ate was around noon and I'm voraciously hungry (remember my eight months pregnant status.) I'm thinking about how I now need to find 'Holy Redeemer' without an address and get set up within 30 minutes while the guests are sitting in the pews. I'm thinking about how convenient it would be to find a parking space relatively close to the church since I have over 60 pounds of equipment that I now have to lug all at once rather than on a couple of trips. I am thinking about how this could be the beginning of the end; my first wedding ever missed because the wedding coordinator confirmed the wrong time. I am hoping that I don't get a speeding ticket for the NASCAR moves I am making out on this highway.

I got to the suburb in 20 minutes flat. I stopped at a gas station for my directions. I first consulted the local phone book to get the address and then asked anyone within earshot where the address was located. Some people looked at me with blank expressions and another was kind enough to respond with, "I think it's down the street." Once the cashier was not busy, they confirmed it was "down the street" and over by five blocks. I was back in the car at lightning speed (or as fast as a pregnant woman, who is freaking out, can move in the heat of July.)

I made it to the church after navigating around some dead-end streets and one-ways, and sure enough, found that I was not going to find a parking spot in this residential neighborhood. The church didn't have a parking lot and the majority of the guests had already arrived. With all the time spent trying to find the church, I had just 20 minutes to set up before the bride walked down the aisle. I threw caution to the wind and parked in a 'no parking' zone and raced inside with all of my equipment. (Once again, the term 'raced' used loosely with the physical and mental state I was in.) On the verge of tears and collapsing, I set up in record time. The one coordinator whom I would have normally spoken with caught me as I was racing around and asked me why I was late. I informed her that her colleague had given me the wrong start time and that only by a stroke of pure luck had I looked at the invitation to find the address and then had seen the correct ceremony time. If I hadn't looked at the invitation when I did, I would have continued to sit in line for my food and then driven down the highway at a respectable speed. By the time I would have arrived at the church, I would have missed the wedding.

The other coordinator did admit that she had accidentally confirmed the wrong time with me. Apparently, the time of the wedding had changed two months earlier because it was thought the original start time was going to be too late. I also asked the 'accident' coordinator to please go out and move my car to a different parking spot which was not in a tow away zone. She was kind enough to oblige. I think she saw – and understood the torment I was in by the crazed look in my eyes. The rest of the event went just fine and according to both coordinators, the bride and groom didn't even notice. Whew!!!

Here's another good one to get the blood pressure elevated. Once again, going by the contract which was confirmed, I set out for a wedding and was running early because of that extra 'fudge' time I build in to my schedule. I arrived to the church, brought in my equipment and started to set up. I was contracted to be there early enough to catch some pre-ceremony coverage. When I was done with some basic setting up of tripods, etc. in the sanctuary, I took a camera and set out to go find the couple and the bridal party getting ready in the basement. When I got downstairs, it quickly became apparent the bride was the wrong bride!!! I asked if there was another wedding going on at this particular church and was told they were the only wedding at this particular church on that day. Time to have a heart attack! I had now spent close to 30 minutes at the wrong church though it was the right church according to the contract.

This, of course, would have to happen at a time my cell phone wasn't working (my 2-year old son felt it would be good to give my phone 'swimming lessons' the day before.) So, to continue...

While I was setting up at the wrong church, the bride's sister called our office wondering when I was planning to be at the church. (Thankfully, my assistant was still at the office and hadn't yet left for his wedding, that day.) He told her that I should be at their church by now and pulled the duplicate copy of the contract to confirm with her that I was due at St. Michael's Church by 10:30am to catch pre-ceremony coverage. That's when she told him that there was a last minute change in plans since St. Michael's had double booked the day. Then she added, "You would have known this if you had looked at the invitation we sent you two months ago." My assistant then explained to her that we work off the contract with all of our notes and pertinent/confirmed information on it, the same information that both she and the bride had *confirmed just a week ago*, as it was documented on the contract by me when I had spoken to them.

But back to me wondering where my bridal party was now located... The pastor hadn't yet arrived to the church and no one else was in the office... After my assistant got off the phone with the bride's sister, he immediately called the police department of the suburb where St. Michael's church is located. He got the dispatcher on the line and asked if she could send a patrol car over to the church to find me to tell me I was at the wrong church. The dispatcher said they would get to it when they could. As soon as he hung up, I got through to him on one of the phones of the 'wrong' bridal party members, and he told me what had happened as I confirmed that I was definitely at the wrong church. He gave me the correct info and I was on my way. By the time I arrived to the correct church, I was only 15 minutes late for the pre-ceremony coverage (thanks to that 'fudge time'), and apparently the photographer had the same mix up with the couple. Wouldn't you think that if you had planned something important, such as wedding, you would make sure that everyone knows where you're going to be?!?!?!?

Back in 1991, early in the business, a bride called me one Saturday and said she was getting married the following Tuesday morning at 11:00am, and would like me to come out and videotape it.

During the conversation and the contract process, I had confirmed the day with her at least five different times. I was new in the business and in my excitement, had forgotten to ask the important question, "What's the address of the church?" Maybe it was the fact that the wedding was taking place on a Tuesday morning that had side-tracked me from remembering that question. Anyway, Tuesday rolled around and I set off to the church with an address from the phone book. When I got to the church, there was no one in sight. It was 9:45am. I thought maybe they were running a little late so I sat in the car for a bit, waiting. At 10:00am, one car pulled into the parking lot and a man got out. I walked over and introduced myself along with telling him I was there for the wedding taking place, that morning. Along with looking at me as if I had lost my mind, he informed me that he was the pastor and there was no wedding scheduled for that day. Oh great! If there was a wedding somewhere, I am at the wrong church... And if there isn't a wedding, someone pulled a great one over on me!

Exasperated, I showed him the contract and asked whether or not I was in fact at 'Hope United.' He said, "Yes, you are. But there is no wedding scheduled today." He then added, "Wait, there is another Hope United two miles away. We are Hope United Lutheran, and the other one is Hope United Methodist." He called the other church and confirmed for me there was, indeed, a wedding there that morning. I thanked the pastor and once again, tore out of the parking lot at break-neck speed to get to the other church. I arrived at 10:20am and had enough time to set up before the 11:00am wedding. The couple understood the mix up and apologized for not giving me the full name of the church, or the address. Everything turned out well, and that was the day I did my first and only Tuesday morning wedding!

There is yet another bridal couple who didn't bother to tell me their ceremony time. I had just dropped off the kids at the daycare facility and drove to the church at a law-abiding speed. When I arrived, I noticed there were a lot of cars, but I was after all in a residential area on a Saturday afternoon and again, there was no parking lot for the church. I wheeled my equipment into the church and thought to myself that they sure had a lot of relatives there for the picture taking time. I was five minutes into setting up when the church wedding coordinator came over and started to reprimand me for setting up late. I told her that the ceremony wasn't going to be starting for over an hour and I would definitely be done by then. She pointed up in the balcony where the organist was ready to begin playing the pre-ceremony music while the guests were going to be seated. She then informed me that the ceremony was going to be starting in 20 minutes whether I was ready, or not. With no time for a nervous breakdown, I quickly finished setting up the front-remote camera and then the balcony camera. With seven minutes to spare before the processional began, I found the bride and groom. While I was placing the lapel microphone on the groom, I asked the couple about the change of the ceremony start time. The bride told me the time had changed the previous weekend and with such a small number of guests, they just called everyone to let them know about the new time. Just as I was about to say that no one called me, the bride added, "The photographer told me that he would take care of calling you to make you aware of the new time and that I didn't need to worry about calling you; he would do it." By the smile on my face and the sweat dripping off my forehead, they had both correctly come to the conclusion that he had not called me.

Fortunately, everything went well with that shoot, too. I did find out later that the couple questioned the photographer about whether or not he had called me. He claimed that he had just gotten too busy before the wedding and didn't have a chance, but figured the couple would have called me, anyway. Based on his flippant answer, the father of the bride did not pay the photographer the last third of his payment. Guess what goes around, comes around...

Ceremonies

Over the years, I have been to many weddings and most ceremonies take place with few, if any, mishaps. All of the couples, for whom this statement holds true, are very pleased. There are some wedding ceremonies, however, that don't go according to plan no matter how much planning was done...

Who Invited Mother Nature?

We'll start with weather-related incidents. All of the weddings in this category happened in the great State of Minnesota and as all of us who live in this great State know, you can never accurately predict the weather in Minnesota. It's similar to Forrest Gump's observation: "Life is like a box of chocolates; you never know what you're going to get."

I shot a wedding in 1991 when the night before the wedding day, 3 to 5 feet of snow fell on the Twin Cities and surrounding area. From where I lived, it would have taken around an hour to get to this wedding with decent road conditions. Phone lines were down due to the storm and I was unable to call the couple to check on the status of the wedding. So, with the contract and directions in hand, along with a road emergency kit, extra food and a lot of blankets, I left for the wedding.

The ceremony was scheduled for 4:00pm and I left my house at 9:00am, not sure on how long it would take to get there... _If_ I was going to get there. It took 5+ hours to drive 45 miles. I plowed through snowdrifts higher than my car, hitting top speeds of 15 mph, but gosh darn it! I made it to the ceremony!

When I got to the church, it looked like the entire building was a snow drift. I could see the roof and the small bell tower and that was about it. By the time I arrived, it was around 2:30pm and the brother of the bride, who was parked at the church on his snowmobile, was directing anyone who might show up to go directly to the reception hall. When I arrived there, I found the bridal couple doing their best to keep smiles on their faces, distressed parents of the couple, one set of grandparents who lived nearby, the entire bridal party who had come into town the night before, a few guests, and the photographer who had also managed to get there on his snowmobile and, along the way had picked up the Pastor. That was it. The reception hall included a huge dance area that had been set up the day before, to accommodate a reception for over 300 guests. By the time the makeshift ceremony started at 4:00pm, at the reception hall, there were 63 people in attendance. For the most part, everything went according to plan. The dinner was taken care of because the owners of the reception hall, who also served as cooks, wait staff, and clean-up crew, lived right next door. The food for the reception had been delivered and prepared the previous day. The photographer and the videographer were there and the florist did deliver the flowers. Although the majority of the guests could not attend and there was a lot of left-over food, the music was great; the brother of the bride, substituting for the DJ who couldn't get there, played from his own collection.

In a neighboring town, a decade later, I shot a wedding on a beautiful June afternoon. Although a blizzard wasn't on the radar, a severe thunderstorm (which turned into a tornado) did appear. When I arrived to the church, the sky was blue and dotted with fluffy white clouds. The temperature was hovering just above 90 degrees. I was contracted to be there for the pre-ceremony coverage activities and with the weather being so beautiful, the majority of the photography was done outside. By the time the picture-taking was coming to an end, the sky to the west was looking ominous. When the processional started, the rain started. Hail came with the Readings, and by the time the Homily was to start, the tornado sirens had already sounded. Everyone in the sanctuary was herded into the basement and I quickly grabbed all the equipment I could, as did the photographer, and we headed into the basement, with everyone else.

After the sirens had stopped and people were allowed back into the sanctuary, the ceremony picked up where it had left off. Heading outside, people were confronted with branches and debris strewn everywhere. Later, at the reception, I heard that there was, in fact, a tornado touchdown a little over a mile north of the church!

While the majority of my bridal couples have played it 'safe' with Minnesota weather, I have worked with a number of rebellious couples who have opted for outdoor weddings, nonetheless. There is almost always something that goes awry at these events.

A few years ago, I had a bride who was adamant about having an outdoor wedding. It started to sprinkle towards the end of the pre-ceremony photography and then it let up when the ceremony had begun. During the ceremony, the guests, bridal party, and pastor would often look up at the sky. Right after the vows, a downpour suddenly started and people were running for their cars. Fortunately, I was using common sense going into this ceremony. I had both cameras wrapped in plastic (sensitive, electronic equipment does not fare well in the rain) and I had my other equipment covered with two umbrellas. When the rain started, I zipped up my equipment bag and moved both cameras and the bag quickly into the sheltered picnic area where everyone else, who had not run for their cars, was standing. The ceremony continued in the picnic shelter.

Of course, there is the opposite end of the weather spectrum: The 'beastly-hot-with-no-relief-in-sight' day. Along with the guests not faring well, this weather is also a 'no-no' for sensitive, electronic equipment. I always feel bad for the men who are all dressed up in tuxedos and standing in direct sunlight – it's bad enough being in a stuffy church with no air-conditioning. There have been a few weddings where the couple gave some thought to their guests' comfort. One wedding had their service program printed on handheld fans. Another wedding served lemonade to their guests before and after the wedding. (The only consideration here would have to be whether public restrooms were readily available. Remember: Drink responsibly!)

For the 'cautious' rebels, there is always the tent option although, some of those decisions have had their drawbacks, too. One day was windy beyond belief and although the tent and the side walls sheltered the guests, the wind hitting the sides of the tent made it impossible to hear anything; they were heaving in and out like bellows. There was another ceremony under a tent which did not have the sides down. The wind, that day, sped through the tent and around the guests, as if it were a wind tunnel. Before you ask... no, the unity candle at this wedding definitely did not light. No matter how many people, and how many hands they grouped around the unity candle, it was not going to light.

The same wedding that survived the 'wind tunnel' effect had more problems, later in the evening. When the bride realized the wind was not going to stop and the wedding still had eight hours of reception time left, she had a family member call the tent company to have them bring out the tent side walls – that was good. At the beginning of the dance, however, it started to rain and that's when people started noticing the leaks in the tent roof. The water wasn't gushing in; it was more like pin prick holes. Every 4 to 6 feet, there was another leak, a force of nature that made for some interesting dance dips.

Another wedding, which had a water problem, was one I shot a few years ago. This one actually was a 'gusher.' Throughout most of the day and evening, there had been a steady rain – a good soaker. This is great for a farmer's crop, but not good for an outdoor wedding. The couple did have a tent with side walls but, going unnoticed, water was collecting in pools on the roof of the tent. Towards the end of the night, the ground had become so soaked that the tent pole, at the corner of the dance floor, sank into the wet ground and collapsed from the weight of the water. Once this pole went down, it created a 'domino' effect and took the tent poles, on either side of it, down too. A 144 square foot area of the tent came down and covered half of the dance floor as well as all who were on it. The revelers out on the dance floor didn't seem to mind very much. I think the combination of earlier drinks and a collapsing roof just added to the fun. No one was too distressed. The DJ, however, was thanking his lucky stars that he (by choice) had decided to set up in the opposite corner and, fearing that the tent might continue to collapse, started taking down his equipment, which marked the end of that reception.

In 2001, I did another outdoor wedding at a community park. The couple did not rent a tent and actually, there was no need for one. There wasn't a cloud in the sky. It was beautiful; beastly hot, but beautiful. As a matter of fact, the pre-ceremony footage I shot at their wedding was used on my last demo – just beautiful. While I was setting up the cameras and equipment for the ceremony, it was still sunny – not a cloud in the sky. When the guests started to arrive, though, the clouds moved in in full force. I had checked the weather earlier and there was to be no rain so, I didn't bring umbrellas. I did have my plastic wrap and white cotton hand towels to protect the cameras from direct sunlight but none of this would help if it started to rain. What was to have been a 40-minute ceremony was sped up to just shy of 25 minutes by skipping some parts. The entire ceremony was encompassed in cloud-to-cloud lightning and constant thunder. It was as if Mother Nature was trying to be patient but really wanted us out of there. I filmed the entire recessional but didn't bother to follow the couple to their getaway car. I packed up my equipment in record time and ran to the car; once again, water + sensitive, electronic equipment = bad mix. There's nothing like going for a run, in a black formal dress, in high humidity. My hair and makeup were already messed up. I didn't need to be rained on, too. As soon as everything (including me) was packed into the car, the downpour started. Oh, did I happen to mention that I was seven months pregnant at the time? Joy.

After the Storm:

The basis of my first scenario would be bugs; mainly mosquitoes. Lots of mosquitoes. Gnats. Biting flies. Did I mention the mosquitoes? Unless the couple during the planning process is wise enough to remember to 'work' with the bugs, bugs will ruin their day. These small, insignificant creatures will just end the fun.

One outside wedding that was just a barrel full of monkeys, or I should say bugs, happened at a site which specialized in outdoor weddings. For a few days prior to the wedding, it rained, and rained, and rained. Not only was there a plethora of bugs, but half the grounds were flooded. Throughout the entire ceremony, the bride, groom, and the bridal party are seen on camera swatting and swiping at the bugs. At times, it was so bad, the groom would swear at the bugs. These words came over the wireless lapel microphone straight into the camera, loud and clear. Fortunately, it was a two-camera shoot so I had another audio source.

The second after-rain wedding happened in the backyard of the bride's parent's house. All her life, she planned to be married in her parent's backyard and nothing was going to deter her from this goal – not even the rain which had fallen for six days straight prior to her wedding day. The backyard was just a mud pit. The white guest chairs and the ceremony riser looked neat and clean before the guests arrived. All the pictures were done on the deck and patio prior to the ceremony. However, when the guests started to be seated, the chairs started to sink into the ground. Guests, especially those with high-heeled shoes, started to sink into the ground. A few guests found that when they were walking to their seats, the mud would suck those shoes right off of their feet. People were tripping and catching themselves on other guests, lurching those guests forward onto sinking chairs. When the processional was to begin, the aisle runner was rolled out and that was the last time it was ever going to be white again. After the 10 couples of the bridal party traversed the runner, each couple sinking the runner further into the mud, it was the Bride's turn. By the time she took her Groom's arm, her beautiful white dress had a six-inch black border at the hem.

Shhh! Keep Quiet!

I have caught many unexpected noises during wedding ceremonies. Once again, no matter how much planning goes into the event, there are just some things that are beyond the control of the couple. Some forethought can, however, prove helpful.

With the stunning landscaping and flowers, the Lake Harriet Rose Gardens in Minneapolis are a popular stop for bridal parties and photographers. Sometimes, people have their ceremonies in the park, too. They will plan a lovely wedding amidst the beautiful roses with a string quartet, meaningful readings, a personalized homily, touching vows they wrote themselves and memorized, and will have invited only their closest relatives and friends to share this experience with them. The only thing they failed to take into consideration is the fact that the Gardens are under one of the busiest landing flight paths of the Minneapolis-St. Paul International Airport!

The entire wedding I shot there was filled with jets coming in about every 15 seconds. Those planes were so low you could read the numbers on the tails. Every time the noise of one plane would start to fade, another plane would show up. This is one couple who was very happy they hired a videographer who had both a wireless lapel microphone on the groom and another microphone plugged into the amplifier/audio system. Personally, I don't think the bride and groom even heard each other until they were able to watch their ceremony video on television.

Another ceremony that you would have to watch on a television in order to hear anything would be the same one that served lemonade to their guests on that beastly hot day (in the park with no public restrooms.) This park is located on a busy bay of Lake Minnetonka. (Actually, any part of Lake Minnetonka is busy, especially on a Saturday afternoon, in July.) The wedding was held so close to the lake that all anyone could hear were boats and jet skis. No pun intended, but the entire wedding ceremony was 'drowned' out by watercraft.

Finally, another wedding that had noise issues was one held the same day as a small town celebration. Part of the big event included a parade and the church was unfortunately located at the end of the parade route. The ceremony started at 3:00pm and so did the parade. About 10 minutes into the ceremony the parade started to come by. For the remaining 20 minutes of the ceremony, all that was heard were bells, horns, fire engines, bands and cheering people. Their wedding day proved to be quite the celebration! Although they weren't all invited, the entire town joined in the festivities; they even had a parade for the couple!

Animal Magnetism

Great title, huh? Actually, animal magnetism is not what you might think it's about. It's about how family pets and other animals are involved in the ceremony. (Tsk, tsk for thinking otherwise...)

Did you know live butterflies are shipped for weddings and other special events? The first time I saw this was at a wedding in 1998. It was so cool! Everyone got a little decorative box on the way out of the ceremony. When the bride and groom left the ceremony location, everyone opened their boxes and the sky was filled with butterflies! As a matter of fact, that same 'butterfly' wedding, which was an outdoor wedding in Shakopee, MN started off with the bride and her father arriving at the aisle runner via horse and carriage. It was a warm evening with lovely weather and a beautiful sunset during the ceremony. She planned well.

While we are on the subject of releasing winged creatures at the end of ceremonies, dove releases are a popular touch. I have seen many of these and all of the releases were quite successful - except for one. The parents of the bride thought this would be a nice touch and arranged the release of doves as a surprise. Typically, the bride and groom will each hold a bird and release them at the same time, but since this was both a surprise for the couple and the bride harbored this 'thing' about birds, it was planned that the release would be done behind the bride and groom as soon as they walked out of the church.

As planned, the bride and groom walked out and 10 doves were released. The groom and especially the bride were startled and the crowd "ooohed" and "aaahed" and nine doves flew away gracefully. One bird, however, hadn't successfully planned its flight path. The aerodynamically-challenged bird flew right into the bride's cathedral length veil and then the excitement really started. It was a remake of the Alfred Hitchcock movie 'The Birds' right there on the church steps. The bride was shrieking hysterically and running around as if her hair was on fire. The bird was doing its best to flap free of this crazed human being but was just getting further entangled in the veil with its claws and beak. Meanwhile, the parents were trying to restrain the flailing bride to get the veil and headpiece off her head so the bird could free itself.

After what I'm sure felt like an eternity for both of the bride and the dove, the headpiece and veil were off her head and the bird was untangled and safely put back into its cage. A word to the wise: Always think through a plan before you surprise people.

There are two other ceremonies where animals were actually a planned part of the day and not a surprise. Both weddings used dogs in the processionals and the recessionals. One dog was the couple's yellow Lab that pulled a custom-made cart up the aisle with the ring bearer seated in it. Another couple had a family friend who owned a miniature Chihuahua that didn't mind being dressed up. For this special event, he was dressed in a tuxedo and top hat and was considered the honorary ring bearer. He even had his name printed in the service program!

Ceremony Happenings

This particular ceremony almost happened in a chapel of a Twin Cities' hospital. Just shy of a week prior to the scheduled wedding date, the Father of the Bride had a heart attack. The first call I received was the day after informing me of the families' first decision to postpone the wedding. Two days after that, I received another phone call saying the wedding was back on and going ahead, as scheduled, and the Bride's Father could watch the video in lieu of being at the ceremony and reception. The morning of the wedding, I received yet another call from the Groom at 7:00am telling me to be at the hospital's chapel rather than the church so the Bride's Father could attend. At 9:00am, the Groom called again, relieved that he had caught me before I had left and informed me that the wedding was switched back to the church.

It turned out that some 'strings were pulled,' and the Bride's Father was allowed to attend. The Mother of the Bride escorted her daughter down the aisle, and two pews short of the Groom, the Bride's Father was allowed to accompany his daughter and wife the rest of the way (with his IV tree) for him to place his daughter's hand into his soon to be son-in-law's hand. Not a dry eye in the place. After the ceremony, the Father of the Bride, his IV tree and the two nurses, who were part of the deal, went back to the hospital.

Over the years, I have also been hired by some of the nicest people you would ever be lucky enough to meet for Interfaith, Interracial and Commitment weddings. I have also done a couple of weddings where siblings will share their wedding day with each other. In other words, rather than having only one couple up on the altar, there will be another one or two couples up there. I can see where that would be very economical if you were one of many siblings from a large family. Of course, I have also done two and three weddings, from the same family, within a 12-month period. The most difficult responsibility for this situation falls on the parents, not only financially, but also with having to come up with a special and personalized toast to the couple. For example, if you have two daughters who get married within five months of each other, the parents can't say at the latter wedding, "This is the most beautiful wedding we have been to." The toast has to be original. The parents just can't use the same toast and change the names. I would have to imagine that this situation presents a lot of pressure. My kids had better not do this to me!

Over the years, my youngest bride and groom have been 17 and 19, respectively. Sadly, the bride was dying of terminal cancer but was able to marry the love of her short life, and get her wedding day giving her parents and relatives the honor of attending her wedding celebration.

My oldest bride and groom were 83 and 85, respectively. Although both of these weddings were special, I was especially honored to videotape the wedding of this older couple. They were 'fond of each other' in high school, 68 years prior, but life had sent them on their separate ways. Each of them had been married once, had a family, and both widowed. Somewhere along life's path, they bumped into each other and picked up where they had left off 68 years before.

Their courtship was brief and their wedding was a huge celebration among their two families. These two people were overflowing with so much joy - it was just wonderful to be there. Apparently, they had done such a good job the first time around with love and marriage, 'fate' gave each of them another chance.

"I Do" Productions had always advertised that we were willing to travel although a nominal fee could be incurred depending on the location. I have shot weddings in Iowa, North and South Dakota, Wisconsin, and of course, all over Minnesota. But I would have to say that the most exciting location I was ever hired for was Walt Disney World, in Florida. Personally, I had been there multiple times, but it was exciting and unbelievable that my company was hired for a wedding that would have palm trees, and Mickey and Minnie Mouse on the video!

It all started at a bridal show. A bride and her 'entourage' stopped at my booth and fortunately did not ask, "What do you do?" They asked me about my different services and prices, and then asked if I was willing to travel. I said, "Sure. Where's the wedding?" I was fully expecting the bride to bring up a location 20 miles, or so, outside of the metropolitan area when she replied, "Walt Disney World." Now came the question which I knew was just going to put a kibosh on this possibility... I asked her for the date of her wedding. Instead of giving me a date I was (most likely) already booked for, she said, "Thursday, November 6th, of this year." I practically shoved the contract into her hand, and jokingly said, "Sign right here!" My impatient wait for November had begun.

Now as a parent, I was faced with a real stinker of a decision: Do I go for just the wedding and leave the family at home? Hmmm... Two or three days without the kids... The idea had merit. Or, do I take the kids and turn it into a family vacation? Well, I knew that I would be a 'bad parent' if I left the kids at home. Plus when you live in Minnesota and have an opportunity to go to Florida in November, you don't just go for two days. Nope, you live it up and go for ten days!!!

Well, the morning of our trip arrived. Our flight was scheduled to leave at 8:00am, which meant (back then) we had to be at the airport by no later than 6:30am. However, with all the cameras, and equipment, and luggage, and two kids, and their luggage, and the two car seats, and the stroller, and the 'whatever-you-do-don't-forget-the-anti-boredom-kids'-travel-bag,' we had to be at the airport no later than 5:45am – which was a real treat for all of us because we are not morning people. I can only imagine what we looked like lugging all that stuff down the concourse to the gate.

Their wedding day started with some footage of the groom and the groomsmen getting ready at their rented villa. After some of that footage, it was off to the Grand Floridian Hotel to videotape the bride and her bridesmaids. When the bride was ready to depart for the ceremony, she boarded Cinderella's glass carriage, complete with the four plumed white horses, a driver, and a footman. The four-camera shoot of their ceremony was at the Wedding Pavilion on the Seven Seas Lagoon. The reception dinner was held back at the Grand Floridian where both Mickey Mouse and Minnie Mouse made their appearances and entertained the reception guests. After dinner, I followed the Bridal Party over to Fantasia Gardens for a round of miniature golf. The fantastic day was topped off by an evening stroll out on the boardwalk over to EPCOT for the Illuminations Fireworks display, miniature desserts, fresh fruits, wedding cake and petits fours. If you're ever invited to a wedding at Walt Disney World, don't think – just go!

Weddings in 1995 were those of the fainting brides. During June and July that year, five of the brides who had hired me, fainted standing on the altar. Two fell on the floor, one fell on her groom, one fell on the priest, and one fell on her maid of honor. They just fell over. Seriously. I don't know if it was heat or stress. Maybe they hadn't had a thing to eat that day? I don't know, but it had appeared to be an epidemic.

In 1997, I arrived for a scheduled wedding, brought my equipment in and walked over to the couple to introduce myself. I told the bride that it was nice to finally meet her in person after spending so much time talking on the phone. She looked at me and asked, "Who are you?" I said, "Well, like I mentioned, my name is Kiersten and I'm your videographer from 'I Do' Productions." She looked at me with a puzzled look so I asked, "You are Sherri, aren't you?" starting to worry that I was at the wrong church. She replied, "Yes, but I don't know who you are." Again I said, "I'm Kiersten... The videographer... You hired me to shoot your wedding. We have talked a number of times on the phone and we just spoke again a few days ago." I then asked, "Don't you remember?" She quizzed me one more time with, "What do you do again?" Exasperated, I showed her the contract with her signature on it and said, "I videotape weddings with a video camera. You hired me."

Suddenly the light bulb came on, "Oh! That's right! I hired a video person! So nice to meet you," she said. I replied with, "Nice to meet you, too. I'm going to go set up." I was glad to leave and continue with my set-up. I'm going to assume she was stressed and I'll leave it at that.

An assistant and I shot a wedding in Becker, MN, back in 1992. The wedding took place in a small country church. And when I say small, I mean small! It was kind of like a toy church. A trial-sized church to see if everyone liked it; the problem, though, was no one ever built the regular-sized church. I think that church has truly been the smallest church I have ever been in. It was cute. It had six pews on either side of the center aisle from front to back. This church was literally 20' x 20'. Needless to say, this church was always crowded.

The only place to set up the back camera on this 'beastly-hot-with-no-relief-in-sight' day was dead center at the back of the church where my assistant sat on the window sill, directly under the bell tower rope. When the ceremony was finished, my assistant stood up and we both heard an awful tearing sound. Both of just knew the seam of his pants had ripped, and started panicking as to what we were going to do for the rest of the day; we had to get straight over to the reception, but he needed new pants. I had him, inconspicuously turn around so I could (nonchalantly) see how bad the damage was – see if he could get away with the damage without upsetting the planned schedule for the day. Instead of a tear, I told him there was something crusty on his pants, and then I looked at the window sill to see if he had sat in something. It turned out that when he got up from sitting on the window sill for 45 minutes in the heat, he had pulled up three layers of varnish now stuck to his pants. Oops!

Any processional with a ring bearer and/or a flower girl always has a chance of something happening. In fact, it's inevitable with young children. As for the kids, they know how to 'work' this situation to their advantage. They get a 'party' atmosphere all weekend long, and they get to dress up and have people fawn all over them. Most importantly, they get presents and if they work it just right, they get a lot of presents before the weekend is over. The 'Master Toy Plan' (MTP) begins at the pre-nuptial dinner where there is a disbursement of bridal party gifts. The first toy is scored – a thank you from the bride and groom for being a part of their special day. Little does the couple know, from the child's point of view, the couple is coming in second with the advantages of the weekend.

The wedding day brings another score for the 'MTP' with an acquisition during the photography, prior to the ceremony, to be good for those few hours and to not get the wedding outfit dirty or damaged. At the time of the processional, another acquisition is promised as it is dangled at the end of the aisle, like a golden carrot. Now depending on the age of the child, this golden carrot can range from being a box of animal crackers to money. Pertaining to the money option: The older the child, the larger the denomination of the bill to a certain value. More may be awarded at a later time for overall behavior during the weekend.

At the reception, the 'MTP' falls by the wayside and is easily replaced by punch, candy, cookies, cake, and more candy, etc. The next morning, however, it's back to business at the gift opening. If all has run smoothly, and according to expectations, another acquisition for the 'MTP' may be gained, as an overall thank you for involvement in the weekend. A child could easily attain 3 toys, $20.00, and one heck of a sugar high all in 48 hours. Not bad pay for someone so young!

The longest elapsed time for a processional due to the number of attendants would be the one where there were 20 – count 'em! 20! 20 attendants on each side!!! What did this couple do? Call 'Attendants – R – Us' and rent people to fill out their bridal party? There were 43 people on the altar! Forty attendants, the couple and the officiant... Holy bridal party, Batman! Placing a front camera for that wedding was very difficult. For the processional, they just kept coming, and coming, down the aisle...

The longest time for a processional that can be charged to the way the attendants walked up the aisle would be a wedding I shot in Minneapolis. There were nine attendants on each side, and each couple did the 'step and stand' routine all the way up the 100-foot aisle while sort of grooving to the organist's jazzy, gospel processional music. One couple at a time – and I emphasize, one couple – grooved and stepped and momentarily stood all the way to the front of the church before the next couple was even allowed to step onto the aisle runner. This processional took a little over 20 minutes!

Once the processional was done and the ceremony way underway, that's when the "Hallelujahs", the "Amens," the "Amen Brothers," and the "Mmmhmmms!" started. These would happen at any time throughout the ceremony from any one of the guests who'd raise either their hand or their handkerchief in the air and voice their approvals. The best part of this wedding, however, was the full gospel choir. Talent flowed in abundance from this group! Their voices were absolutely beautiful! Wow! Simply wow! This choir should make an appointment at a recording studio. Are there any Agents/Managers out there?

Logic demands that if there is a *processional*, there must naturally be a *recessional*. Back on July 4, 1992, however, our groom was either studying to be a preacher, or was already a preacher. And when I say 'preacher', that boy knew how to preach! During the homily, he took the Bible from the officiant, turned around and started talking to the congregation. Following his apparent aspiration to become the next television evangelist, he started walking back and forth, in front of each pew section holding up the Book of Scriptures and then started down the aisle, leaving his demure bride, up on the altar, by herself. The entire time he was walking, he was telling stories and quoting scripture. Occasionally, he would stop at a pew and pull an unsuspecting guest out of their seat and raise their hand in the air. He came down the aisle so far that he was within 10 feet of the back camera and momentarily directed his efforts into the camera. He was red, and sweating, and every muscle in his face was flexed. He then walked back up to the front and fell to his knees, raised the Bible into the air, and hung his head down. In the silence following, the officiant quickly took the Bible from his hand, and moved the ceremony onto the vows. Everyone in that church was stunned.

One of the services I provided was something called a 'Picture Retrospective.' Basically, it's a video montage of baby through engagement photos with an overlay of audio memories chosen by the couple. Often, these retros will be played at pre-nuptial dinners, receptions, gift opening, etc. Occasionally, they are played at the church typically right before the ceremony starts. A few years ago, we had one bride who decided to just this, at the last moment.

When this couple received their finished picture retrospective from me, they loved it and couldn't wait to show it to everyone else. They had a TV brought into their pre-nuptial dinner and everyone enjoyed the unexpected entertainment. The next day, at the ceremony, the couple decided to surprise all the guests at the ceremony and project the picture retrospective up on a 12' x 12' screen in the sanctuary, which would have been just fine except that it was 3:00pm on a sunny day and the sanctuary had many skylights including one right above the screen. After the ceremony, the bride approached me and angrily said, "You made the picture retro wrong! It worked just fine last night, but no one could see it today!" I reminded her that there was a large skylight in the ceiling, right in front of the screen, and with that much light coming in in front of the picture, no one was going to see anything. I then assured her that the picture retrospective would still work, just fine, on any television or screen so long as the sun wasn't shining on the picture. Her relieved response was, "Oh, okay. Thanks."

There is, of course, the other side of the coin: Couples who prefer the dark. That 'romantic' dark lit only by candles, a.k.a. 'cave' dark. Unfortunately, in that light, no person and no camera will ever see anything clearly. I have had many couples who have chosen to have this 'romantic mood-lighting' and then when they watch their video afterwards, wonder why everything was so dark? I've explained to all of them, prior to the wedding, that the human eye is many times better than any camera will ever be; if a human eye cannot see well in a certain type of light, there is no way a camera is going to be able to 'see' anything. As a matter of fact, last winter, I taped a wedding that was so dark, the officiant laughed during the ceremony and said, "I apologize, but I seriously can't read my papers. Does anyone have a little bit of light? Perhaps, a tiny flashlight?" Needless to say, this couple did not complain when they received their completely dark video.

At the end of ceremonies, couples will typically give each other a kiss. Ah, the kiss... For those of you who have already been through a wedding ceremony, I hope you did a nice job on the kiss. For those of you who have yet to be married, when that day arrives, I hope you will remember that the kiss should be a 'church kiss.'

First of all, remember to kiss. I have had a few couples who are so anxious to leave the ceremony that they completely forget this little detail. Now, when I say little, I don't mean a quick peck. It should be a warm, tasteful kiss that all of your guests will be comfortable with and one that will look good on film, both the photography and the videography. By no means should it be an 'eat-you-face-off' kind of kiss which makes your guests want to blush. I have seen post-ceremony kisses that have made me question whether or not the couple was actually in love, or even knew each other prior to their wedding day? Of course on the flipside, I have seen kisses that didn't really qualify as 'kisses'... They were more like maulings at the end of ceremonies which made guests squirm, parents gasp, and officiants look horrified. And dear groom, if you want to be a bit outrageous with the kiss, you can always go for that romantic dip. Just don't drop your bride... I've seen that, too. (Doesn't go over too well...)

In 1992, I did a formal military wedding at the Cathedral of St. Paul. The groom's family was of Irish heritage so the men were attired in kilts, including the groom. The couple was serenaded by a few bagpipes while leaving the ceremony, and descending the front steps of the Cathedral. The groom's fellow officers made an arch of 16 swords that the bride and groom had to pass through on their way to their vintage limousine. At the end of the arch, one of the officers (un)ceremoniously tapped the back end of a very surprised and embarrassed Bride, with his sword. That exit remains particularly vivid in my memory as the brilliant midday sun was lighting the front of the St. Paul Cathedral, the air was filled with the pomp and circumstance of bagpipes; vivid colors, smiling faces... Beautiful!

Finally, one more way to end a ceremony: In 1995, I had one couple who were both police officers, and had met each other while attending school. They ended their ceremony with a nice kiss and then hand-cuffed themselves together before they walked out of the church to their 'getaway' car!

Rings & Vows

When it comes to the rings and vows, most people will repeat the words after the officiant. A good portion of these couples, however, are so nervous that they forget to look at their spouse-to-be and continue looking at the officiant while they repeat their vows.

Then there are some people who are daring and memorize their vows. One couple did just that and added some personal requirements to their oaths. While it surprised the officiant and the guests, Mike promised to help in the preparation of meals, not watch sports on TV 24 hours a day, and give her foot massages when she had a long day at work. Allison added that she would clean up the kitchen anytime he cooked, would try to curb her spending habits, and would give him a back rub when he had a long day at work.

Sometimes a wedding ceremony has a best man who wants to be a comedian or worse, all the groomsmen want to get in on the act and pretend to lose rings. When the time arrives for the best man to hand over the wedding rings, all the groomsmen look at each other with the puzzled look of, "Who has the rings?" Some will even go so far as to search through their coat and pants pockets, or walk over to a seated guest and retrieve the rings. Not many brides find this to be funny, though, and there are fewer officiants who see the humor.

Of course, there is the extreme version of the 'where are the rings' scenario, albeit it's usually an accident. Most often, the rings are left in the ring box which is in the bag of 'stuff' in the bride's room, downstairs. Of the three times I have seen this occur, twice someone else's rings were used as a substitute and the other time, the ceremony was halted until the rings could be found.

Another memory I have about rings involved a wedding I shot at Hennepin United Methodist in Minneapolis. At the time the rings were to be handed over from the best man, they were accidentally dropped. Those two rings hit the wooden floor and took off. All of a sudden, the entire bridal party except the bride, who was standing there with a very unhappy look, dropped to the floor and started searching. The rings were found (one had rolled 10 feet away), and the ceremony continued.

Lastly, in the late 90s, two clowns got married to each other... Yep, literal clowns. They weren't dressed in their professional attire, but they did exchange rings suitable for their profession. The Groom's ring squirted water (the water being held in a balloon which he held in his hand.) A 5" plastic daisy covered the Bride's entire left hand, and came with an attached bumblebee which darted around the flower when her hand moved. I don't know if they had 'traditional' rings, but these rings certainly made for colorful and humorous pictures!

Light My Fire... Or Not

The very first wedding videotaped by "I Do" Productions, back in 1990, was done at no cost to the couple so footage could be obtained for demonstration purposes; a 'demo' video. For the ceremony, a two-camera shoot was offered (one in the balcony and one up front, off to the side of the altar.) Although the second (front) camera was also offered at no charge, the groom was sure that they only needed one camera in the balcony.

Their wedding day arrived, and the one camera was set up in the balcony for the ceremony. I wired the groom with the lapel microphone then went up to the balcony and waited for the ceremony to begin. Everything went perfectly: No camera troubles, the tripod movements were fluid, the microphone was clear throughout the vows... "I Do" Productions was going to have a great demo video to show prospective clients!

After the vows, the Unity Candle Lighting was the next order of business. The couple picked up the tapers and held the flames to the unity candle wick. Nothing happened and that's when their beautiful ceremony video and my demo video ceased to exist... The couple started digging the wax out, from around the wick with their fingers in an effort to get the candle to light, and when that didn't work, the groom started swearing – every four letter word in the book! Since I was new to the business, and the groom demanded only one camera, I didn't have the audio source a second camera would have provided. Of course, I also never would have anticipated that part of the ceremony was going to turn into a swearing-fest. The groom swore through the majority of the song which was sung during the 'lighting' of the unity candle and although he was really quite creative in his word groupings, the candle still did not cooperate.

Over the years, I'd say close to half of the unity candles did not light, or had some trouble lighting. Most of the wicks would burn rapidly into the candle and become covered, immediately, with wax. Some didn't light because of the air currents in the church which were caused by air-conditioning, fans, or windows which were opened. As for outdoor weddings, the percentage of successful unity candle lightings plummets drastically!

Another wedding I shot out at Hennepin United Methodist provided an interesting unity candle experience. I had the front camera up on the altar, hiding in the front choir area, on the far side of the unity candle. The couple successfully (at first) lit their unity candle and the camera caught their loving smiles. Before the couple turned around, however, they witnessed the flame go out. That's when their faces became horror stricken and they both started gouging at the wax to get the wick unburied. Their candle never did re-light but, fortunately, the front camera had captured the first attempt. (This couple fortunately chose to have two cameras at their ceremony. They were smart.)

Lastly, there was the service folder that alerted the guests to the 'Lighting of the Unity Cow' after the vows. Someone had not proofread their work. You can only imagine what the bride thought of this error...

Getaways

I will first start off with two brides involved in getaways. However, they weren't leaving ceremony locations, they were leaving gas stations. The first bride, I overheard at the church while she was getting ready, drove away from the gas station and forgot her credit card. She had one of her friends retrieve it later.

But a friend of mine did one better on her wedding day. She pulled into the station, pumped the gas, went into pay, got back in her car and drove away... With the pump nozzle still in the car! Oops! She said she heard this clunk and looked out the side mirror to find the nozzle lying on the ground. She reversed, fixed the problem, apologized to the station's owner, and then left. Fast.

One couple from St. Paul was driven to their reception courtesy of a 1932 fire engine; the 'royal chariot' of the St. Paul Winter Carnival's Vulcan Krewe. I can't recall if the groom was a Vulcan, used to be a Vulcan, or was related to/friends with someone who was a Vulcan but they were transported to their reception via 'Luverne', the

Vulcan Krewe's beloved fire engine. A handful of Vulcans, dressed in their finest ceremonial garb, participated in the colorful (and loud) getaway, as well. Quite the sight!

Speaking of St. Paul, another wedding took a llama cart from their ceremony to the reception. I heard later that the City of St. Paul was not happy about this; traffic control with cars is one thing. Llama carts is quite another.

A couple in Anoka left their ceremony site on a dirt bike. Apparently, the groom was a National Motocross Champion and brought his bike to the church for pictures and the getaway. Their reception was in St. Paul though so, at the bride's request, I'm sure, they only went a few blocks on the bike and had a limo take them the rest of the way.

One couple from Eden Prairie, MN called in a helicopter to take them from their ceremony location to their reception out at the Lafayette Country Club. They held this bit of information a secret from everyone. During the ceremony, they looked at each other and giggled a little bit when they heard the helicopter arrive. The rest of the guests, however, just thought they were sharing a special moment. The surprise worked! Kids were jumping up and down, and running in and out of the church carrying on about a helicopter out in the parking lot while people were moving through the receiving line, inside the church. The couple exited the church, kissed each other and waved goodbye, then climbed in and flew off into the cloudless, summer's day.

I have had many couples leave their ceremony locations in modern and classic limousines, Bentleys, Rolls Royces, Model A's & T's, rebuilt classics, and sports cars ranging from BMWs to Corvettes, to Ferraris. There's a specific memory I would like to interject here: In 1994, one of my couples walked out of their church and the getaway car was a brand new Corvette. The bride looked quizzically at the groom and all he said was, "This is my wedding gift to you," and handed her the keys. (I can't remember what I received from my husband as a wedding gift, or if we even exchanged wedding gifts. But I do know that I did _not_ receive a brand new Corvette!)

Anyway, I have seen stretch Humvees and Navigators, a stretch '54 Chevy and stretch limousines: One with a chandelier, one with a hot tub, and one with a rumble seat. People also leave in horse-drawn carriages, hay wagons, horse-drawn sleighs, or by boats on trailers hauled by trucks, complete with the fishing pole props along for the ride. We are, after all, in Minnesota – Land of the 10,000 Lakes, or in some cases, loons!

For all the wedding receptions I have ever done, I have always made an effort to get to the reception before the couple in order to catch their arrival. Once, as I was coming up behind the limo transporting the bridal party, I noticed some material hanging out of the window, and it was flapping around in the wind. The limo was in the right lane and I was approaching in the left lane. As I passed, I realized that I was looking at the rear end of a bridesmaid, and it was the hem of her dress blowing around.

She was mooning everyone on a major thoroughfare around the Twin Cities. When the bridal party arrived at the reception, everyone was quite secretive about whose butt was hanging out of the window. Fortunately, I was driving rather than videotaping, at the time.

For this memory, I will not name any suburbs, people, places, times or dates because this couple was escorted by a fire engine which led their limousine to their reception. The groom was a fireman and his buddies at the station did this escort for him and his new bride complete with bells and horns when the truck should have been at the fire station in order to be ready at a moment's notice for any call that might have come in. I learned later that such an escort was a rule book 'no-no,' and to never utter a word of it to anyone, ever. See? I can keep a secret!

Pregnancy & Videography

No, this chapter is not what you think it's about although I'm sure I have shot a number of weddings for couples who were already a 'threesome.' Actually, this chapter is about my personal experiences of being a pregnant videographer. (I have four children which means, I have 40 months or a little over three years' experience on this topic.)

I will start with my daughter, my first child. When my belly started to protrude, and it happened rather fast (she was a big baby), I found it increasingly difficult to stand next to my tripod. Typically, I stand between the tripod legs and can look into the viewfinder, straight on. The longer I was pregnant, and the bigger I became, I found I had to arch my upper torso in a rather awkward and uncomfortable fashion in order to see into the viewfinder. It finally reached the point where rather than standing between the tripod legs, I would have to sort of side straddle the tripod and stretch to see anything.

"I Do"

After I started feeling her move at about the fifth month, I noticed as all mothers do, she would sleep as I was constantly moving around (my motions were lulling her to sleep) and when I stopped, she would wake up and start moving. Well, when shooting a ceremony, I'm not exactly jumping around in the balcony so she'd wake up. A few times she would deliver a powerful kick that would bump the tripod leg, and therefore, the picture. Try and explain that to the newlyweds, "Um, my unborn baby kind of like, kicked the tripod and made that bump in your picture. The baby says she's sorry." Thankfully, most weddings used two or three cameras so if there was unexpected movement, I could switch to another view in the editing process.

Once I figured out that I had to stand to the side of my tripod, all was well with my four pregnancies in regard to 'kicking the camera.' I also learned that babies enjoy classical music. During processionals, musical selections, communions and recessionals, there would be no movement, whatsoever. However, during the readings, Gospel, homily, ring exchange and vows, it would be party time. When each baby came home from the hospital, I would play classical music for them at bedtime, and it worked like a snap; out cold. As all of my children have grown older, one of their favorite types of music is classical and no, they don't always fall asleep when they hear it now.

Fortunately, my daughter arrived in June which meant I didn't have to suffer throughout the entire summer like I did while I was pregnant with my three boys. Doing anything at temperatures over 50 degrees Fahrenheit while pregnant is tough; shooting a wedding is just sheer torture. The stress, lugging all that equipment, getting in and out of a car... Put it this way, I don't miss it.

Let's not forget about trying to stay ahead of the couple and getting the shots, etc. while carrying another human around. Actually, I am reminded of a wedding I shot out near the border of Wisconsin in 2000 with a photographer who was also pregnant. Both of us were only a month away from our due dates. The couple was more than accommodating when it came to catching them on film as they left the church. They wanted to run out of the church and hop in the car and leave, all within 30 seconds. Bless them; they were kind enough to wait for us to waddle out of the church and get into position for the shot. Both she and I were waddling as fast as we could all over the place that day. I'm sure it was just hilarious to watch.

The other 'joys' of being pregnant include being voraciously hungry, pretty much, 24 hours a day. Although churches and synagogues frown on food being in the sanctuary, eating when you are hungry – especially when pregnant, keeps away the dizzy and faint feelings, lessens the nausea, and keeps the stomach from grumbling – all situations which ideally should be avoided while shooting a wedding ceremony! There have been several times when I have packed a little lunch for myself and have continued eating in the balcony through an entire ceremony. You know, lean down to look at the pew and pop a grape and a cracker in your mouth, or 'dig' in the equipment bags and eat half a sandwich while doing so. I don't think anyone ever suspected that I had a one-person buffet up there.

The other 'joy' of pregnancy, of course, is having the need to visit the restroom, often. Actually, the word 'often' really doesn't describe the situation. It's more like I should have just lived in the bathroom. Besides the agonies of being in the middle of one-hour ceremonies, or two hours of nonstop toasts during dinner, or four hours of constant action on the dance floor, I'm reminded of a wedding I shot at a private residence. The ceremony had finished, I had my equipment packed and in the car, but I really needed to use a restroom before getting out on the road. I walked back into the house and the mother of the bride directed me to the first door on the right, down the hallway. I rushed to the bathroom and thankfully found it unoccupied. I opened the door and yes, it was a bathroom with all the fixtures including a floor-to-ceiling, wall-to-wall window. The entire wall was a window and the toilet was right next to it!!! I desperately searched for curtains, a shade, blinds, something! I hurriedly walked back out of the bathroom and again sought the mom of the bride to ask if there was a hidden curtain in that bathroom or something I was missing, or perhaps another bathroom I could use that did not have a huge window looking out onto a backyard where all 200 guests were sipping champagne and nibbling on canapés two feet from the toilet?!?! I was dying; my eyes were starting to water. She calmly assured me with a light chuckle that it was a one-way window. I rushed back to the bathroom, closed the door, and then proceeded to make funny faces and gestured at the window to see if anyone would notice. After assuring myself that no one could see in, I finally relaxed. But good grief! When you have to take care of business and there's this huge window next to where you sit and you can watch party-goers chit chat, eat, drink, and have a gay old time adjacent to you – it's very disconcerting. In retrospect, it was funny; but absolutely unnerving, at the time.

During each of my pregnancies, if there were two weddings booked on a day, another crew would take the wedding which required either more time or had more locations, stress, or special requests involved. Two months before my daughter was due, I was meeting with a couple whose wedding was coming up the following weekend. Compared to the other wedding scheduled for their day, this one was a walk in the park: Lutheran wedding, four hours total at the event, and no guest interviews; easy and a perfect shoot for me. When I arrived for the appointment and they saw me, they promptly told me that they didn't want me at their wedding. I asked them what the problem was and they said they didn't want a pregnant woman at their wedding. They asked if I had another crew that could shoot their wedding instead but I told them that everyone was already booked that day for different events. Then they demanded either a different crew shoot their wedding or they wanted a full refund. They also shared with me their disappointment that I had 'let them down.' I explained to them that I was scheduled to do their wedding because they had fewer locations and less time scheduled than the other events for which everyone else was already confirmed. They didn't care and the bride actually told me she was 'afraid of pregnant women' and if I dared to show up at the church, she wouldn't let me in. The tense (and odd) five-minute meeting ended with an ultimatum from the couple: Either another crew does their wedding, or they get a full refund.

I checked with the wedding coordinator whom they had hired. She confided in me that she had been having a lot of problems with them, too. I decided it wasn't worth the trouble, and I didn't want to make things more difficult for the wedding coordinator who referred the wedding to us (thanks), so I switched weddings with my Assistant. The wedding I wound up shooting that day was a 1+ hour Catholic wedding with a few hours of pre-ceremony coverage. After the ceremony, the couple had pictures out at the Lake Harriet Rose Gardens. Per the contract, I followed them to the Gardens to get some footage. I parked right behind the bridal party limo, put a sign on my dash that read, "I am videotaping a bridal party for a few minutes in the park," left my flashers on and told the driver who was standing by his limo, "If any cops show up and want to tow my car, let them know I'm with the wedding." Then I waddled as fast as my swollen ankles could carry me over to where the bridal party was taking pictures.

I returned to my car in less than 10 minutes and had a parking ticket stuck under my windshield wiper. I asked the limo driver why he hadn't told the meter maid that I was with the wedding party, and with a chuckle, he told me it wasn't his problem. Thanks a lot! When they left the Rose Gardens, the couple decided to go bar-hopping – that's always a ton of fun for a pregnant woman!

I did call the Minneapolis Police Department about the ticket. I asked them why it was okay for a limo to park in a no-parking zone, but not cars? I was told that it was because the limo is part of the wedding party. I explained to this person that although I didn't have a limo, I was the videographer and part of the bridal party, too. I also explained that when a couple decides to do some shots at a park, they are usually there for less than 15 minutes and with the huge lack of available parking out there, I didn't have time to drive around looking for parking spots. I also did not have the time to see if any spots were available in the small parking lot at the opposite end of the park. I finished with the fact that a sweating pregnant woman carrying 30 pounds of equipment can only move so fast to catch the constant, never-ending activities of her contracted wedding. I talked the fine down to $10.00 and fortunately, I have never had to go back to the Lake Harriet Rose Gardens.

On June 19, 1993, I was exactly seven days away from delivering my daughter. I was hired for both a ceremony and a full reception that day. The reception was held at North Oaks Country Club. When it came time for the dinner, my assistant and I stood back until everyone found their seats, then looked around for two available seats and were about to sit down when someone on the catering staff rushed up to us and said we were not invited for dinner. I smiled and pointed to my burgeoning belly and said, "I have been busy shooting this wedding since noon and right now, at 8:00pm, I am very hungry and I'm sure you can understand, and my assistant would appreciate a meal, too." She replied, "The bride has requested that both of you leave the dining room. Now."

We had already made an unplanned spectacle of ourselves – the last thing I ever wanted to do. I looked up at the head table and found that the beginning of the dinner was being put on hold until our conversation was done and the 'situation' resolved. My assistant and I grabbed the tripods and cameras and left the room. We were in the hallway for only a few seconds when the father of the bride came out into the hallway and said that although I wasn't invited for dinner, I was to videotape all of the toasts, etc., and whenever nothing was happening, I could go back out into the hallway and wait.

I followed the bride's father back into the room to tape the blessing and some toasts and noticed the photographer and his assistant sitting at a table having a great time and eating their four-course meal. When I returned to the hallway, my assistant and I were approached by another staff person who offered us 'box lunches' (code for stale, cold sandwich, one soggy pickle, and three potato chips.) We thanked her for the offer and told her that any food would be greatly appreciated. She then told us the box lunches were $10.00 each. Neither my assistant nor I had that much cash on us, so we sat there with no food. We had started shooting at 12 noon and we left there at 12 midnight with nothing to eat the entire day. (Pregnant and eating for two? Heck, I would have been happy eating for one!)

During the dance – which, of course, I was taping, I asked the photographer how he managed to get a meal and not be kicked out of the dining room? He said, "It's all in the contract, Darling. They have to provide me a meal, in the dining room, with their guests." The very next day, the fine print about a meal being included found a permanent spot on the "I Do" Productions' contract. By the way, did I mention that the father of the bride was an OB/GYN doctor?!

On July 10, 1993, I shot my first wedding since the birth of our daughter. The photographer at this particular wedding kept looking at me, all day, with a puzzled look on his face. Finally, at the reception, he approached me and asked, "Weren't you pregnant? Like a month ago, when I saw you at another wedding? You were pregnant, weren't you? Maybe it wasn't you." I confirmed his suspicion and replied, "Actually, yes I was pregnant and I delivered two weeks ago – a beautiful baby girl." And with a deep inhale, he replied with, "Congratulations! Women are definitely the stronger of the human race. Wow!"

Other 'Professionals'

Before we start, please know I have nothing against anyone out there in the great big wedding world – although it may seem otherwise. I give everyone a chance and a lot of times; multiple chances. Let's start with photographers.

When I arrive to a wedding, I introduce myself to the church coordinator, wedding coordinator (if there is one), the officiant, the photographer and I say "hello" to the couple and/or their immediate family. Then I stay in the background. I'm just there to observe the wedding day with a video camera. That's it. But some photographers (I don't know the percentage) just don't like videographers or any other cameras on site including those belonging to guests. I think there are a number of reasons why: They might feel that videography poses somewhat of a threat to photography, although it doesn't. If you think about it, who is going to frame a videotape/DVD and hang it in their living room? Another reason might be that they feel video will cut down on their re-order business. (Actually, the photographer we had at our wedding was coaching us as we were nearing our date on how to get our parents to order at least $3,500 in reprints. They didn't.) This was the reason he was shouting at our guests and relatives during our pre-ceremony photography. Have you seen a reprint of a picture off a video from the 90s? Even after it's de-interlaced, perhaps color-corrected, and printed on the best consumer-priced printer out there at that time, it still didn't have the quality of a photograph from a Hasselblad (film/digital) camera. I think the poor souls were being a bit neurotic.

The first photographer story is about one with whom I dealt with back in 1992. I have a little, 50-watt halogen light attached to the top of my camera which I use during receptions to light the often dimly-lit rooms. Every time I moved to get a shot, this photographer's full head of curly hair would get in the way. He was within three to five feet of me the entire night. I would move to the side, and he would move to the side. I would extend my arm and hold my camera up in the air and aim down to catch some action and he would stick his flash in my picture. I couldn't shake him, the entire evening. A week later, I met with the bride and groom at her father's house. I had explained what had happened, and we watched through some of the reception footage. All of them were appalled at what the photographer had done. He had literally ruined their video. The father got up from his chair and exclaimed, "Well, if he thinks he's getting paid anything past the deposit we have already paid, he's dead wrong!" I have never seen that 'professional' at any other weddings/events since then, and I've done a lot over the past 16 years.

During the photography session of another wedding, while I was setting up my equipment for the upcoming ceremony, I complimented the photographer on one of his shots. I told him that it was a unique pose and from what I had seen so far, it looked as if the photographs were going to turn out very well. He looked at me and said, "Oh, these pictures won't be any good." With concern in my voice, I asked, "Why? What's wrong?" He answered me with, "This bride isn't beautiful. These pictures won't be great." I was blown away. First, the bride was about 10 feet away, and her relatives were all over the place. And secondly, every person is beautiful inside and out, with the possible exception of that particular photographer; he was neither.

I didn't talk to him for the rest of the day and did my best to avoid being anywhere near him. Towards the end of the evening, during the dance, it was very obvious that he was drunk and I had heard from some of the guests that he had slapped a bridesmaid, earlier. I didn't see that happen, but the bridesmaid was nowhere to be seen. I should also say that I am truly amazed that this person manages to stay in business. I know he's been sued many times and the way he acts at weddings is just inexcusable.

"I Do"

At one wedding in Rochester, before the bride got into the limo with her groom, she turned around and said to her particular photographer, "Don't bother coming to the reception. I'm done with you and your behavior. I would like to enjoy the rest of my day, and the only way that's going to happen is to not have you near me." The photographer had a dumbfounded look on his face. He simply turned around and walked away. I still have no idea as to what happened?

I have had the 'pleasure' of working with another photographer who is just unbelievable. Another one of our crews had worked with her two weeks before I shot a wedding with her so, I knew who she was and what (most likely) was going to take place. During the event, two weeks earlier, my assistant was hired for pre-ceremony coverage while she was doing pre-ceremony photography. (Pre-ceremony for us is all the stuff that happens other than the formal photography because, let's face it, how exciting is it, really, to watch people say 'cheese' and stand motionless on a video? Really exciting, let me tell you.) Anyway, my assistant was talking with the groomsmen about a shot he wanted to get with them after they were finished with their photography shot which was coming up next. The photographer turned around and said to my assistant, "Leave my sight immediately!" and then said to the bride and groom, "I don't even know why you hired a video guy when you hired me. Unless your hired video guy physically leaves the building, I am not going to continue my work." She then sat down on a nearby bench and set her camera down next to her. There was a stunned silence in the room. No one knew what to do. The last thing anyone with 'I Do' Productions would ever want to do at a wedding is to be noticed. As a matter of fact, we pride ourselves on going unnoticed and, in the meanwhile, doing one heck of a nice job. Taking the higher road, my assistant quietly excused himself from the room. He didn't leave the church as the photographer had demanded, but instead set his equipment up in the sanctuary to be ready for the ceremony. The mother of the bride followed him and apologized for the unexpected and rude outburst. Fortunately, he had managed to get quite a bit of pre-ceremony footage before his progress was halted.

I have found that in this business, most people aren't used to seeing a female videographer. I have been mistaken for a soloist many times which is terribly funny because I cannot sing... at all. Alley cats sound better than I do! Or, I get, "Are you the florist?" or "Are you the pianist/organist?" or "Are you looking for the photographer?" Or the best one, to date: I was hauling some of my equipment into the balcony when the mother of the groom noticed me and asked, "Are you the photographer's assistant?" "No," I answered with a smile. "Well, don't touch all that expensive photography equipment, I don't want to be responsible for you breaking it at this wedding," she said to me as she was walking toward me to shoo me away. I explained to her that I was the videographer and her son and daughter-in-law had hired me for the day and she said, "Oh! I'm sorry. I didn't know there were any female video people. Do you know how to operate this stuff?"

Anyway, two weeks later, it was my turn. The same rude photographer with whom my assistant had to deal with was shooting pre-ceremony pictures while I was catching pre-ceremony footage. She didn't realize I was hired probably because I was female and I was getting along with the bride and a few of her bridesmaids whose weddings I had shot in the past. Everything was going along just fine for about an hour into the pre-ceremony coverage until the photographer asked me to straighten the bride's train for a pose. I was taping some other people at the time she requested this of me and that's when the bride said, "Oh, she's our video person for the day." "Well, I'm sure she could be a Personal Attendant for a little bit, too," said the photographer with a condescending tone. I was starting to walk over to straighten the dress and keep the 'charade' going. That's when the bride took a stand and said, "No, we hired her. She's a professional videographer." The photographer just lost it. The bride and her parents were watching this person have a conniption fit in front of them. She then spun around on her heels and glared at me. She shoved her camera into her assistant's hands and shouted at me, "You lied to me! You said you were just a friend!" I stated matter-of-factly, "I never said anything to you except 'Hello.' I never lied to you. You assumed that I was a friend." The photographer walked out of the room as she bellowed over her shoulder, "Get her out of here! She's ruining your pictures! Who in their right mind hires a video person?!?!?"

I was certain I had enough pre-ceremony footage so I excused myself and went into the sanctuary to begin setting up. During the ceremony, the photographer took every opportunity to stand in front of my camera, bump my tripod, hiss at me about how stupid video was, and to call me a liar. Fortunately, she wasn't at the reception very long. What a pleasant individual? Such a lovely lady... More like a 'party pooper diva!'

Every time I shoot a wedding, I always suggest to the photographer that we share the center of the balcony or the aisle so we can each get a 'center' shot. Most photographers are fine with this arrangement and appreciate the thought. I should also include, there is a 'rule' regarding the proper position for camera placement in the center aisle: Cameras should be placed in the aisle behind the last seated row of guests so as to not obstruct the view of people attending the wedding. It's a common sense, and professional rule.

Well, in 2002, I worked with a photographer in Prior Lake, MN who agreed to share the aisle (the church had no balcony.) As soon as the bride and her father walked down the aisle, the photographer picked up his tripod and camera, and followed them right down the aisle! Right in the middle of my shot! Thankfully I had the front remote camera, but I didn't get the shot of the back of the bride's gown nor her arm in arm with her father. I also did not get the back camera view of the father placing the bride's hand in the groom's hand. The shot from the front camera was blocked by the best man with where the couple was standing at the time so, instead, I got a great shot of the back of the photographer! Another bit of wedding video ruined by a photographer. I figured he was, at least, going to move his butt back down the aisle after he got his extreme close-up, but no. He set up camp 15 feet off the altar! He was smack in the middle of the aisle, standing among the seated guests. It was a packed church that day and he had at least 20 pews, on either side, behind him. During a solo, I quietly walked up from behind him and whispered, "What in the world are you doing up here? You should be in the back of the church... as we discussed." "You had a good idea," he whispered back, "But I think that I have a better view from up here." "You're blocking all the guests' views," I said. "Well, they can look around me," he said. I had no other choice, if the video was going to be of any value. I walked back to my camera, picked up the tripod and walked back to where the photographer was standing. I set my tripod next to his and said, "You're not a professional photographer, are you?" He didn't answer me.

Later, I found out he was the neighbor of the bride's parents and he worked as a photographer for a catalogue; setting up shots of chairs, tables, lamps, shoes, etc. The bride and her family, obviously, didn't take into account that photographing a pair of shoes in a closed studio is different than shooting a wedding in a church. Apparently, he gave them a good deal on the price.

Okay. Enough on the photographers... I could tell you endless stories about photographers at receptions for example, the ones who insist that I move because, after several moments of deliberation on their part, they believe I am standing in the perfect spot for 'their' shot whether it be for the cutting of the cake, or the garter and bouquet toss, or the father of the bride's toast. Whatever the shot, I always seem to be in the perfect location for *'their'* shot! The old saying, "The grass is always greener on the other side," holds true for many photographers. But, let's leave them with their cameras.

Do you remember the DJ that I mentioned from my own wedding? Mr. 'I-couldn't-remember-the-names-of-my-clients-if-my-life-depended-on-it' so-called professional DJ? At every wedding I have shot with this DJ since my own wedding, he has always managed to forget the names of the couple. Wouldn't you think after one embarrassing reception where you forget your client's names, you would put a little extra effort into remembering future client names? Apparently, this important fact of customer service is not on the top of the list for some; it might not even register on *his* list.

In 1996, I was shooting a reception at the St. Paul Hotel. The bride's and groom's names were similar to 'Kristine Pahl and Patrick Timms' (names are changed for privacy.) Anyway, it was time for the first dance, and I said to my assistant, "How much do you want to make a bet that the DJ is going to not remember the couple's names? I bet he's going to mess up the introduction." Sure enough, the couple strode onto the dance floor with elegance, and the DJ said, "We're here to celebrate with..." and he started frantically shuffling through his papers, "A wedding reception for... Kris and Tim!" Upon hearing the wrong name, the bride's smile turned to a frown and a guest tiptoed up to the DJ and whispered, "No! It's Patrick!" The DJ's reply, on the microphone with shock in his voice, was classic, "This reception is for Patrick and Tim?"

Another DJ who I worked with a few years ago came to the reception with some faulty equipment. Later in the evening, the couple had started their 'Dollar Dance.' Both the bride and groom with their respective, temporary dance partners were each four feet away from the DJ's set-up. All of a sudden, the top framework holding the mirror ball and lights crashed to the dance floor. If anyone would have been one foot closer to the DJ, they would have been conked on the head. There were shrieks and gasps on the dance floor but the music continued and the DJ rushed around to the dance floor and picked up the framework.   With the help of another guest, he fastened the piece back onto the upright frames. Thirty seconds after the DJ got back into position behind his console, the framework fell again. Thankfully, no one was nearby or got hit.

Speaking of reception entertainment, at the beginning of the "I Do" Productions adventure, I was shooting a reception at a country club on Lake Minnetonka.   The entertainment for the reception was a smooth, low key, jazz band which, I thought, was great. Unfortunately, this band was hired by people whose idea of a successful reception was to have guests stand around and converse with each other, eat hors d'oeuvres and take full advantage of the open bar. The ballroom was packed with people, wall-to-wall. By the end of the first hour, I had shot everything there was to shoot and I still had five hours left on my contract. There was a cake cutting to be filmed but no one wanted to be interviewed on camera and there was no first dance. Actually, there was no dancing at all.   Not once during the entire six hours of that reception did anyone do anything that resembled dancing except maybe for the tipsy walking of individuals moving from one group to another group, or the people who misjudged where a chair was and fell on the floor.

"I Do"

It was dark, boring (from a service person's point of view), and stuffy. The band had been hired to play from 6:00pm to 12:00am; three sets with two breaks. Their second break came at 10:30pm and that's when they had finally had enough - they started packing up their instruments. The father of the bride panicked and asked what they were doing. I think the father agreed with the band that it was pointless to stay because he offered them an additional $1,000 on their contract to remain until midnight. They politely refused and left anyway. About a half hour later, some of the guests started to leave and that's when the bride came up to me and in a wobbly state said, "Yuh did fantasti-job. Yuh can leave when yuh wan. Yeah. I thing yuh got everythin." I said, "Thank you and congratulations. Call me when you get back from your honeymoon." As I turned around to leave, one of her guests bumped into her and spilled red wine down the front of her gown and they both burst into laughter. Quite frankly, I don't blame the band. I was scratching at the doors an hour and a half into the reception to get out of there, too.

The worst 'professionals,' however, would be the ones we have referred and turned out to be 'no shows.' In November 1992, I had referred a couple to the bakery I had used for my wedding. Their wedding was on a Friday night and the reception was at Union Depot in St. Paul. They had confirmed everything with all of their vendors including this bakery. Sure enough, the cake was not there when they arrived and they couldn't reach anyone at the bakery because it was closed for the day. The bakery had done such a nice job on my cake and cakes for other weddings I had referred. I was embarrassed by this particular referral, however, and apologized profusely even though everyone involved knew it wasn't my fault. Lee Ann Chin had a restaurant in the building and the manager was kind enough to provide dessert for the couple to split and feed each other so we still had that traditional video shot. (For fun, take a wild guess about when the wedding cake finally showed up at the reception site. Did you guess the following afternoon, on Saturday? If you did, you would be correct.)

I have also referred couples to different limo companies; four, to be exact. The first company I referred didn't show up at the wedding site (the cake fiasco all over again.) The couple hitched a ride to the reception with the bridal party members.

The second company I referred did show up to the church with a classic car to pick up the couple, but drove only about a mile down the road before breaking down. I picked up the couple, in my car, on the way to the reception.

The third company showed up with a limo which was just a mess. The wedding was in early May and apparently the limo had been used the night before for high school prom rides but hadn't been cleaned up before the appointment of picking up the bride and groom, the next afternoon.

The fourth company referred is excellent: Beautiful cars, attentive service, chocolate covered strawberries, and champagne. This was actually the limo company we rented as a surprise for my sister-in-law's wedding night to deliver her and her new groom to their hotel suite since we knew, in advance, they would be relying on friends for a ride from the reception to their hotel. Towards the end of the book, I will tell you more on how they decided to use their gift of a limo...

And don't even get me started on ministers, priests, pastors, rabbis, and ceremony location wedding coordinators. Most of these people are just fine but there are the few ten percent out there who really should be forced to attend a school where courses offered include such titles as, "How to play nice with the rest of society," "Wedding vendors are people, too," and "Although I think I own this church/synagogue, the building belongs to all members, not just me." These people would have to pass all courses with flying colors, gold star stickers, and happy faces before they could be allowed into any ceremony location!

The last 'professional' story that I will leave you with is about a DJ. During the garter removal, the groom took the garter off the bride's leg rather quickly and the DJ said to the crowd, "Boy, the groom is pretty fast there. I sure hope the speed of the garter removal is not a sign as to how the rest of the wedding night will go."   There is bad taste and then there's just plain bad.

Where's Grandma?

There have been a few times when grandparents have disappeared. Nothing bad has happened to them, but they just wind up missing for a little while. The scariest thing about these memories is that they may predict what will happen to me when I become elderly. Oh no!

Some brides and grooms choose to finish their family photo session after the ceremony, before parents, grandparents, etc. leave for the reception. Consequently, this disappearing thing happens quite often. Whether the grandparents were ever informed or simply forgot depended on the communication lines but a lot of grandparents came up missing when the photographer needed them in a shot. They were always found later at the reception enjoying their selves, but also wondering where everyone was...

Speaking of grandparents who get whisked away to receptions, this memory is of a grandma who, after the ceremony in a large church, needed to visit a restroom. Before she was taken to the reception by whoever was assigned to give her a ride, she set off to find a bathroom. Apparently, there was another wedding, which had also just ended, in the small chapel of this ceremony location. When she came back out of the bathroom near the chapel, with her coat on and purse in hand, an overly helpful relative from the other wedding offered a ride to the reception. She accepted the kind offer and left.

Once her family arrived at the reception and were seated for dinner, they noticed that Grandma Millie was nowhere to be found. Panic struck and the blame game of "You were supposed to drive her to the reception!" started between the various relatives. Reaching into the "You think?" basket of ideas, the minister suggested that perhaps she was at the reception of the other wedding, which had occurred at the church's chapel, that afternoon. He and his wife were going to stop at that reception later that evening, and so they had the invitation out in the car. It was retrieved, the other reception location was called, and it was confirmed that they had an 'extra' grandma. Fortunately, the other reception was in a neighboring suburb and the father of the bride went over to collect his mother; she was found sipping champagne and having a lovely time chatting with everyone around her.

In another case, a set of grandparents attended the wrong reception. The reception, for this particular wedding was held at a hotel hosting three different weddings, that evening. When these grandparents arrived at the hotel, they were conveyed along by a group of guests who were moving toward one of the ballrooms. Again, it wasn't until everyone was seated for dinner that the couple and their parents realized grandpa and grandma were missing. Hotel security was notified and a few guests searched the parking lot for their car. Their car, in fact, was in the parking lot but empty, and hotel security checked the public areas as well as verifying they had checked into the hotel that afternoon but they weren't currently in their room. Finally the bride and groom took matters into their own hands and set off to find his grandparents. They decided to look in on the other receptions scheduled that evening and found the dear souls sitting at a table in one of the adjoining ballrooms, talking with guests. The bride and groom for that reception had not yet arrived so they had no idea they were at the wrong reception. Isn't it nice that grandmas and grandpas are so universally welcome at various events?

Reception Revelry

When people ask what I do during the week, I always reply, "We have our videography business during the weekends and we have our black mailing business during the week." I'm just joking, of course, but we get some very interesting footage from these events when people are unaware they are on camera or, in some cases, when people either don't care or they want to be on camera.

By themselves, reception stories could make a very thick book. Every reception "I Do" Productions has ever videotaped has provided at least one memorable happening so they will be shared just as they come to mind – no particular order – kind of like my life.

First of all, I'm going to say I have seen more groomsmen's butts than I ever thought I would see, in the past 16 years! Actually, I wasn't planning on seeing any at all. I will admit the first time a set of groomsmen decided to moon the camera for their interview, I was a bit startled. However, after dozens of these interviews, I've noticed a pattern. The guys decide on their 'master plan,' and then set their beers down. After verbally expressing their happiness for the newlyweds, they all look down the line at each other to make sure they still have a plan and then they all turn around, drop their drawers, and bend over. Well, isn't that a sight to behold!

After they think an adequate time has elapsed for the filming of their back ends, they stand up and turn around while refastening their pants. They all have that 'strutting about the hen yard' look on their faces because not only did they just show their prize-winning derrieres on camera but because there was a female behind the camera. Rather than falling down in a dead faint because of what I had just viewed, I believe I may have upset these fine, upstanding, gentleman when I just picked up my tripod and camera and walked away. Sorry boys... Once you've seen one, you've seen them all!

At this point, I'm going to share three opinions with you. Okay, they are more like pet peeves. If you are in the planning stages of a reception and you follow these three suggestions, you are going to have happier guests and service personnel:

Pet Peeve #1: If you are planning a 'Grand March,' which is basically the introduction of your entire bridal party and yourselves to the guests, please do this at the beginning of your reception as you are entering the room. This just makes more sense to everyone and it's a great way to add fanfare to the beginning of your reception. If the 'Grand March' is delayed until after dinner and before the dance, guests become 'antsy' while everyone in the Grand March is rounded up from the bathrooms, the bar, their hotel rooms, the parking lot, the terrace, or wherever. The guests just look bored. Also, your entertainment for the dance isn't left standing in front of a bored crowd wondering when they should begin the music.

Pet Peeve #2: Stealing the bride and groom. If this annoying tradition just has to be done, please schedule this during the trip to the reception from the ceremony location. Stealing the couple during the reception, typically between the dinner and the dance, is the best way to make sure that your guests will either be bored out of their minds, or will be attempting to achieve some new level of alcohol consumption. Some guests will just leave for the evening because they don't want to stick around while nothing is happening and they don't know what time the couple will be back. They are at the reception for the bride and groom and if the couple is not there, they will leave. Again, the band or DJ would like to start the dance but the newly married couple is missing. And as a videographer, there are only so many interesting shots of bored people.

Pet Peeve #3:

Q) What time should the cake cutting happen?
A) After the Grand March, but before the blessing and toasts.

I suggest this because everyone's attention is already on the couple, since they were just introduced. On their way to the head table, they just stop at the cake table (all eyes are still on them) and they cut the cake, etc. After the photo-op, they can continue onto their table for the blessing, toasts, and dinner. Then while dinner is being served and consumed, the catering staff can cut the cake and have it ready to be served immediately after the entrée. The natural sequencing means the entertainment can begin with the first dance while the guests are finishing their desserts; a perfect segue into the remainder of the evening.

If there is one thing I have learned over the past 16 years, it would be that the wedding day's events itinerary has to be well-oiled and smoothed to perfection. Oh! There is just one deviation from this perfect itinerary: Be sure to allocate a 15 to 20 minute 'fudge' throughout the day, and then everything will be 'on time' and most importantly, everyone will be happy.

Thank you for your time while I cleaned out my opinion closet, and now, on with the show...

Okay, speaking of the planning stage, we had one mother of the bride, years ago, who was having her daughter's wedding at a very posh country club in the Twin Cities. While she was meeting with us to contract for the video services, she was telling us about what plans she had already made and what she still needed to do. Somewhere in the conversation, she mentioned to us that she had 300 guests so she had reserved three kegs of beer, and then came the 'kicker': The country club had charged her $250 per keg! We gently explained to her that one keg of beer, no matter the quality, is definitely not worth $250, and we suggested she renegotiate this expense with the catering manager. Fortunately, she did question the price and saved herself over $600 which she put toward her video. It pays to be kind and helpful.

While I'm talking about it, I have one other story about this country club. Many years ago, two wedding receptions were hosted there on the same evening. Within 10 minutes of each other, the two brides walked into their respective dining rooms and freaked. The elaborate wedding cakes were in the wrong rooms! The bride, for whom I was hired, was a bit miffed that her $1,200 wedding cake was sitting in someone else's reception but fortunately thought of it as more humorous than anything. The other bride, however, went on a tyrannical rage through the country club demanding to speak to someone and looking for the cost of her reception to be refunded. As for that bride's mother, one could tell the bride didn't fall too far from the tree. Together they were carrying on like two howler monkeys, out in the lobby. The club took care of gingerly switching the cakes between the reception rooms and if someone had arrived late, they would have never known the difference. I will add that after seeing that little temper tantrum, I was really quite happy I had been hired for the wedding of the smiling bride.

Continuing on wedding cakes, some of the cutest footage I have ever taken was of children, especially those who don't know they are being watched by a video camera. The true personalities of these kids come out when they are looking at a wedding cake, up close. There are some children who remain standing three to four feet away from the cake table. They have been trained well. There are some kids who will get closer or will stand at the table's edge and say nothing, but the looks on their faces are just priceless. You just know they want to grab a handful and duck under the nearest table, and cram the cake into their little mouths. Some, usually little girls, will stand near the table's edge and point out the intricacies of the frosting and the decorations used such as fountains, staircases, motorized cake toppers, etc. but while never actually touch the cake.

Then you have the kids – usually the little boys – who dare to reach the extra couple of inches and actually touch the cake. These kids are obviously in-training for their future occupations as agents involved in covert operations for a governmental agency. First, they casually walk up to the cake and look around. Some will use the ruse of looking bored and might even walk away with their hands in their pockets only to return within a minute or two. Once they have established that no one is paying attention to them, whatsoever, they will take an in-depth look at the cake: What part of the cake should they touch so no one will notice that the frosting has been tampered with? How thick is the frosting, really? Where are the supports for the cake? (One must be sure it doesn't fall down in the middle of the covert operation.) Which way, through the room, will provide the quickest and cleanest escape route out of the immediate area? One more check over each shoulder to make sure no one is looking... Within a blink of an eye, the crime is done and the perpetrator is gone. The child is back over by the punch bowl just looking at the foil-embossed napkins.

The perfect execution of this mission, however, begins to fall apart on subsequent visits to the cake because either all the precautions are not executed to the nth degree as they were the first time around and/or he has shared his secret indulgence with a select few of his friends, who in turn, have shared the secret with their friends, and so on down the line. Inevitably, the mission is interrupted by an adult and needs to be aborted for the evening. There are also a handful of kids who sidestep the attendant difficulties and just stick their fingers in and take some frosting, no matter who is watching.

While on the subject of cakes, one bride really liked the color green so much that her wedding cake was kelly green. A five-tiered, green wedding cake to honor the Irish groom! These two were a fun couple and very nice. Another fun couple with whom I have stayed in touch had a multiple-tiered wedding cake with frosting that created vertical piano keys. The groom and his family are full of musical talent and the cake was quite fitting for the entire day.

A spectacular wedding cake at a December wedding was frosted in chocolate and trimmed with sugar encrusted miniature cherries, pears, plums, etc. You could smell the cocoa from six feet away! It was just gorgeous!

A lot of the cakes I have seen over the years are just true works of art. One lady I have referred for cakes does 'Austrian Sugar Lace' work on all of her cakes. When she gets to the reception site, she spends three to five hours setting up the cake and attaching, with little dots of frosting, the sugar lace that she has premade. Sometimes the sugar lace is so fine that it breaks and she has to sculpt more, on site, to finish the cake. Now there's dedication and patience. Beautiful cakes... Are you hungry yet?

The last wedding cake story that comes to mind is from, I believe, June of 1998. The couple had ordered a beautiful multi-tiered, marzipan frosted wedding cake. Their reception was in one of the historic mansions along Summit Avenue in St. Paul. Earlier in the afternoon, the cake was set up in a room on the fourth floor, which was the top floor of this location. By the time the couple had arrived at 5:00pm and made their way up to the top floor, the cake was sliding downhill. The top layer had already settled on the table, and the second and third layers were on their way to sliding off. Because of the wooden dowels holding the different layers together, the cake had not yet made it to the floor, but the heat in that room was doing its best to counteract the 'dowel factor.' The wedding reception guests witnessed a cake cutting that wasn't so much a 'cutting' as it was a 'scooping.'

A few times, a groom's cake has been displayed and offered at the reception. One cake had an arrow buried in it with the other end of the arrow lit on fire. Since wheeling around a cake with an open flame was in complete violation of the fire codes, the catering staff followed it with a fire extinguisher in case of any accidents. Thankfully, the flame was snuffed out after all the photography/videography was done and the cake was enjoyed by all.

Another groom was from Texas and his groom's cake was in the shape *and* color of an armadillo. It was about

$2\frac{1}{2}$ feet long and gray and scaly, with glass eyes. When it was cut, we all saw a cake that was literally blood red (lots of food coloring) and with a raspberry filling for the 'realistic' effect. The cake was delicious, but a person has to be pretty innovative to come up with something like that. Actually, if I remember correctly, I think it was the mother of the bride who had come up with this idea! Wow! What a mother-in-law!!!

Have you ever had a banana split cake? (Apologies – it's all coming back to me.) This cake has the bananas, strawberries, chocolate, and pineapple baked right into the layers of the cake, and it's served with ice cream. As a matter of fact, at this particular wedding, the couple had arranged for a miniature, multi-tiered, banana split cake for each table and the couple who had been married for the longest amount of time at each table was responsible for cutting the cake and serving it. Very classy; very cool!

Of course, if you prefer to be over-indulgent and/or don't have too many guests, you can always opt for miniature, individual wedding cakes for everyone. These were a part of an early summer, garden-themed reception (early enough in the season to beat the bugs.) These cakes were terribly cute, and incredibly delicious!

Okay, enough of the sugar high. There have been many locations for the wedding receptions which "I Do" Productions has attended. We have been hired for nearly every hotel in the Twin Cities area, and I know I have been to every country club in the metropolitan area. I have been on both of the St. Croix and Mississippi River Boats as well as a number of the dinner boats out on Lake Minnetonka. We have filmed at the ballrooms of yesteryear, and the community centers of today. And there have been receptions that are beach and pool parties complete with the Luau theme where everyone attends in their best Hawaiian garb and gets a lei. These have had pig roasts, hula lessons in grass skirts and coconut bras, entertainment with flaming spears, and to make it perfect, a musical appearance by Elvis.

I have been in many grand and beautiful historical buildings across the State of Minnesota. I have also been in the beautiful Minnesota History Center, the new Science Museum of Minnesota, the Governor's Residence on Summit Avenue as well as many other historic mansions along that row.

The reception at the Governor's residence took place while Governor Arne Carlson was in office and the groom happened to work with him at the State Capitol. An assistant was shooting this wedding and needed to use three cameras for the ceremony, and then I was scheduled to stop by his reception to pick up an extra camera for my two-camera shoot later that afternoon. Well, I arrived in St. Paul with just enough time to pick up the camera and be on my way. However, I didn't take into account the large amount of traffic and stupendous lack of parking spots! I swear I drove up and down all the side streets and parallel avenues trying to find a spot, but to no avail. I finally parked in a '5 Minute – Customers Only' spot at a drug store a few blocks south and one block east. As my luck would have it, I was now forced to 'hoof' it up a hill as fast as I could on a hot summer's day in a black formal dress and heels to retrieve my camera and get back to my car before the next meter maid left me an expensive present. At last I arrived at the front gate of the residence on Summit Avenue and was greeted by an on-duty State Patrol Officer who would not let me in because my name was not on the list, I didn't have an invitation, and I didn't bring a photo identification. Without completely losing my mind and going nuts on the sidewalk due to continued exasperation, I explained that I was there to meet my assistant and pick up a video camera I needed at a shoot that afternoon. I also added that I really don't have the time to sit around and wait for someone to help me; I need the camera now! Actually, more like half an hour ago would have been better. Once again, I think the crazed look in my eyes told this person that I was not a force to be dealt with; just appease her and she will go away. I had my camera within one minute. I ran back down the hill, careful not to trip on a sidewalk crack with my heels and not to be hit by a car (that would have put a real damper on the day.) I made it back to the parking space and my car was still there. My mission was accomplished; my hair and make-up were a disaster but, I had the camera and I was on my way to the wedding. Oh, the stress! Relax... Breathe in... Breathe out...

I have also taped receptions at the Minnesota Zoo, historic inns and perfectly landscaped gardens, different casinos and lodges/resorts along the North Shore of Lake Superior and in the Brainerd Lakes Area. In 1997, I shot a wedding and reception with a Renaissance theme at Spicer Castle in Spicer, MN. I remember asking the bride about what they were planning to do for extra light, later in the evening when the sun set? She replied that they were going without electricity and once night fell, the event would be complete. That particular wedding was very pretty.

And let's not forget Walt Disney World. Remember, if you are invited, don't think - just go.

One of the most stunning and breathtaking locations for receptions in the Minneapolis area would have to be Windows on Minnesota. The view from the 50th floor of the IDS building at sunset is spectacular and the city lights sprawling out in every direction, especially on a clear night, are gorgeous. The Azur Ballroom used to cater to wedding receptions and special events, too but, unfortunately, that location was turned into a bank. Personally, I think they should have left it as a reception hall. The room was decorated in blues, purples, and fuschia with angular fixtures and, if I remember correctly, a glass block bar. The food was just scrumptious. As a matter of fact, the last wedding I shot there was on May 21, 1994. I remember calling my babysitter to check in on everything and overhearing the initial total of the open bar was at $18,500 and still climbing. Good holy grief!!!

I am reminded of one other funny story pertaining to reception locations. In 1992, we moved to Chanhassen, MN. At the time, the Chanhassen Dinner Theatre was running the play, "I Do, I Do." We immediately started noticing two things: We weren't receiving mail that people claimed they had sent us, and we were receiving mail for the dinner theatre. I called over to their general offices to check on whether or not they were receiving mail addressed to "I Do" Productions and, sure enough, they were. It took a couple of months for everyone involved at the Post Office, and the Chanhassen Dinner Theatre to get it all straightened out. (I imagine they must have wondered, at some point, why people were sending them wedding info.)

I am famous for remembering trivial and useless facts as I'm sure you can tell by now. One wedding where my memory came in handy was for an outdoor, Oktoberfest themed wedding complete with a German band hired from New Ulm, MN. When the bride called to contract us, she introduced herself and started describing the wedding and gave me the date, etc. Somewhere in the conversation, I used my 'memory for useless facts,' and told her it was a small world because of few years earlier, I had shot a wedding for a bride with the same name as hers, and oddly enough, she sort of sounded like that person, too. She informed me that I was not losing my mind and she was, in fact, the same person. She said her first marriage didn't work out (it was his fault and I completely concur) but her Mom loved the video so much, she would still watch it although her daughter was now divorced from the groom on the video; her Mom would just fast forward through the parts he was in. Well, she was getting married again and a new video was in order. The early October weather was beautiful and *everybody* had a good time at that reception!

Before I get any further into the different activities during receptions, I should backtrack a little and tell you one short story about a bridal party getting to their reception. This was a couple who were married in Bloomington, MN and stopped at the Mall of America for some bar-hopping; they hit all the bars on the fourth floor. While they were at the last bar, I asked the mall entry officer if he would stop the bride and groom at the door so I could add a 'joke' shot to their video. He agreed with me that this fun-loving pair definitely looked suspicious, and made them 'assume the position' up against the outside wall of the Mall. You have never seen a gawker's slowdown like this one; both cars, and pedestrians, paused to watch a bride and groom get 'frisked.'

Okay, resuming with reception activities, this reception was on a July 23rd at a hotel in Minnetonka. This was a Greek wedding reception where the groom, towards the end of dinner, stood up and told everyone to drink, eat, and have a great time at the reception. Apparently, everyone was listening quite well. (For a reference point, think the movie 'My Big Fat Greek Wedding' times 10. No, wait. Multiply that movie by 100 times and that will give you a good idea of how this wedding reception was celebrated.) Opa!!!*

*Opa (pronounced 'oopa') is a joyous exclamation commonly used when Greek people are dancing or are in high spirits. It expresses the inner most feelings like saying, "Who cares? Let's enjoy!"

The dance started off well and they did a lot of traditional Greek dancing; a lot of talent in that crowd. As the evening progressed, the guests took to dancing on the tables, the bride was dancing on the DJ's speakers with a dinner napkin tied around her head, and the groom and his groomsmen decided to take it all off down to their (pre-arranged, I guess) matching boxer shorts. Actually, the groomsmen wore red, white, and blue boxers while the groom wore white satin boxers.

The next great idea was to play the song 'Wipe Out' but first the dance floor was cleared of all people so that a few pitchers of beer could be thrown on the floor. Then each groomsman, the groom and whoever else wanted to take part would take a running start and slide on their bellies, across the dance floor, in the beer. If they took their time getting up from where they stopped, a few of their friends would step on their back and pretend to surf, using them as a surfboard.

You have never seen so many security personnel of a hotel emerge from the woodwork! They came out like carpenter ants once the beer hit the dance floor! It was about 11:00pm when that happened and the DJ was ordered to shut down immediately, and the parents were arguing with hotel security that the party was going to continue until the contract end time. The parents told the DJ to continue and security was threatening to pull the plug and there were a few words exchanged. Okay, a lot of words were exchanged.

After the sliding across the floor in the beer, and people calmed down, there was more dancing. Needless to say, when the groom stood up straight his beer-drenched, white satin boxers didn't leave much to the imagination. Eventually, there was a dance between the groom and his grandmother and she took no notice of the fact that those were the only item of clothing her grandson was wearing.

Later, I learned that some of the fixtures were removed from the wall in the men's room during the reception and the dance floor was declared a complete loss. Afterwards, the hotel's lawyers talked with the couple's lawyers and so on and so forth... Good times!

If that sounded like animals in a zoo (sort of like my house), last year, my assistant shot a Jewish reception at Windows on Minnesota, atop the IDS Center, in Minneapolis. Prior to the wedding, there was a running joke between the bride's and groom's families that if he were to take her as his wife, ancient tradition would mandate that the bride's family give two goats to the groom along with the bride – a dowry, if you will. Sure enough, they hired a very efficient wedding consultant who found two goats and two handlers – which was not the hard part, especially in Minnesota. The hard part was when she finagled the Sales & Catering Department into allowing two live goats on the 50th floor of the IDS Center! The goats were a hit – everyone loved them!

Other rarities at receptions, but fantastic entertainment nonetheless, have included belly dancers, flame swallowers, strolling guitarists and violinists. For the children at receptions there have been clowns (these people are great additions to the formal group pictures!), balloon animals (I took a few home for my kids), face painting (yes, I got my face painted, too), magicians (they always leave me befuddled – easy to do, though), a yoyo champion (he was very talented!), and a professional storyteller (she was marvelous!) Oh! I can't forget Santa Claus who brought some special presents for the couple during one December wedding. Santa told them to keep them wrapped until no one else was around. Apparently, they make all kinds of presents at the North Pole...

Hey! A pet peeve that wasn't included in the earlier list: Guests watching sporting events which are televised on the evening of someone's wedding. Record whatever you feel you can't miss at your house, and stay in the reception area when you are a guest! We have been at dozens of receptions where people will filter out of the dance to the bar or their hotel room to watch a sporting event on television, leaving the couple in the ballroom wondering where everyone went.

There was one reception when the Minnesota Twins were in the World Series and out of 350 guests who were present for dinner, there were fewer than 25 left in the ballroom when the couple wanted to do their garter and bouquet toss. Seriously!! I took it upon myself to go into the hotel bar (which was jam packed) and shouted to everyone that the bride and groom needed their guests back at the reception, "NOW!!!" Sure, I got some ticked off, alcohol-induced looks. Some people even told me to, "Shut up and go away." Talk about the pure tackiness of these guests! Please never do this to a friend or relative who has been gracious enough to invite you to their special event. Imagine how you would feel if everyone left your special event to go watch TV? Okay, that was just my

'Mom' personality showing through again... Back to the regularly scheduled programming...

A few other times people sneak out of receptions are when they become amorous with each other during the day's event. We have, trust me, accidentally discovered these amorous people in rooms at the ceremony location where the bridal party gets ready, coat closets of reception halls, cars in parking lots, bathrooms stalls, golf courses at night, and elevators.

Actually, one of the 'coat closet' weddings was at an Athletic Club in Bloomington, MN in the mid-90s. That particular night, there was a severe, electrical thunderstorm that rolled through the area. It was that greenish-black color outside and around 6:45pm the electricity went out. And it stayed out – lightning hit a nearby transformer. Normally, this wouldn't be a problem because a facility would have a back-up generator; this Athletic Club didn't have one. Fortunately, the staff had all the food prepared but to serve a crowd of 250+ people, you need warming lights to keep everything at the perfect temperature while all of the plates are being assembled. The bridal party and their immediate family members were served food which was at the correct temperatures – as it should be. The rest of the guests, however, had entrees that were cold and salads that were warm because it took over two hours to serve the entire crowd.

I would suspect that was the case because there were no lights in the kitchen except for a few flashlights.

Thankfully, as a videographer, all of my equipment was battery-powered; I was good to go. However, the DJ, who was dependent on electricity, couldn't play dinner music or music for the dance. A grand piano was found in the hallway and wheeled into the ballroom and there was a guest who could play piano. Although it was a summer wedding, we were all treated to a few hours of winter holiday music. More than dancing, there were a lot of sing-alongs which I think brought the group closer together. How often do your friends and family gather in one place, around a grand piano in a dark ballroom in the summer, to sing 'Rudolph the Red-Nosed Reindeer' at the top of their lungs? Just when people think a situation is a total loss, there's always another option!

Speaking of sing-alongs, the reception I mentioned earlier – with the frosted piano keys on the cake – had a family sing-along, too. The reception was held at the Marriott in downtown Minneapolis in July of '92. During the course of the reception dance, it was very apparent that both myself, and my assistant were surrounded by very talented people. I remember the band would play a few songs and then various guests in the crowd would jump up on stage and belt out a song or play a few numbers, and then the musicians and singers would change again. The groom was a regular, up on the stage, that evening. I should also say he sang the song, 'Unchained Melody', a capella to his bride during the ceremony and it was flawless! It was absolutely beautiful and I'm sure everyone was awestruck; I was definitely in that category!

The formal reception ended around midnight but the party continued around a grand piano. Since it was 12:30am and I had nowhere important to be at that time (pre-children), I stayed and videotaped the gathering. If I remember, correctly, the groom's parents or grandparents were in Vaudeville Shows and the talent had just filtered down the years with each generation adding onto and honing their craft a little more. It was so much fun to be present at this soiree, time just flew. At 3:00am, hotel security came over and told us to break it up because they were getting noise complaints from the hotel guests. Oops!!! Sorry...

Receptions Involving Water

A couple of years ago, when my eldest son was four years old, I shot a wedding that had a single beta fish in a small glass globe surrounded by seashells and a handful of sand for the table centerpieces, at the reception. At the end of the night, people were urged to take a fish home. I was one of the last people there and the couple knew I had kids so, they urged me to take one, too. Like a good Mom, I took a fish home to add to our happy little family. The next morning, my son was all excited about the new addition and asked where it came from? After I had explained the fish had come from the wedding the night before, he concluded that every subsequent wedding should produce some type of living creature, as well. He would give me a short list of animals to look for during my weddings, and if I saw one, I should put it in my equipment bag and bring it home. If all else failed, I should at least bring home another fish.

There were two other receptions where the table centerpieces used goldfish in glass globes surrounded by ivy, or flowers and candles. From one reception, the fish were not available to take home because they were, instead, going to be taken home by the couple to feed the groom's pet piranha. Yep, that's nice...

As for the other reception, the offer to take fish home never came up because two of the groomsmen made a bet on how many live goldfish they could swallow. I don't know where the count ended, and being such an animal/amphibian/reptile/insect/bird/spider/fish/marsupial lover, I didn't tape the bet. I couldn't tape the bet. Actually, this is the only thing I have ever refused to tape as a videographer in the past 16 years and fortunately, the bride and groom made it quite clear they were disappointed with the two people involved. By the way, I had just trusted my instincts that inclusion of this 'frat dare' would have only served to diminish the entire video.

A lot of hotels have decorative fountains or waterfalls in their lobby, and a lot of weddings have children in their attendance. Just like the description of children and wedding cakes, it's the same thing with children and contained areas of water.

Similar to the cakes, some children stand back about three or four feet and just look; again, well trained. Also, in this situation, a lot of kids have their little arms held onto tightly by their parents to avoid any messy or wet situations. For the kids who are able to get close, though, the call to mischief comes in the form of the coins that are lying on the bottom, just a few inches down in the water. These kids know that if they time it just right, they can dip their bare arm into the fountain and quickly grab at least a few dollars in coins to take along on the next trip to the arcade or use at the vending machines to buy bubble gum and metallic stickers for their bike. All they have to do is roll up their sleeve high enough and make sure no one, especially a parent, is looking. They also need to pick the perfect spot where one quick grab can yield the highest amount. Unfortunately, a fountain or waterfall attracts so much interest that it is hard to remain under the radar. Plus, if all else fails with this opportunity to get into trouble, the challenge of the cake tasting is still at hand before dinner is served.

While we are on the discussion of fountains, one couple had their champagne hour in an open air courtyard location which had a center fountain. This courtyard was solidly filled with people; standing room only. It was near impossible to walk around in the courtyard. As a matter of fact, when I needed to get to the other side for an interview or a shot, I had to re-enter the building and find another exit nearest to where I needed to be, outside. As I was setting up for an interview, I heard a muffled scream from the center of the crowd along with a little splash. I never did see the accident nor do I know which guest it was (she was quickly escorted from the courtyard and to her hotel room so she could change.) I did learn, however, that with a crowd as large as that one, she was inadvertently backed into the side of the fountain and thus lost her balance, and literally fell backwards into the water.

There was another hotel reception which had its champagne hour, poolside. I'm sure you can guess what happened... A guest was carrying some drinks to a friend and was skirting around the outside of the crowd to get where he needed to go. He just happened to be walking behind someone who was telling a great story and using their entire body to emphasize their point. At just the wrong moment, the story-teller jumped backwards with his arms in the air and knocked the guy with drinks into the pool. On the way to falling, he dropped the drinks and grabbed the closest thing he could find to save his balance and that was the guy who had jumped backwards. Both were now in the pool, and not happy. There was shattered glass on the side of the pool and in the pool. The champagne 'hour' had not quite made the hour. Later, as I was leaving the reception, the pool was closed and being drained so it could be cleaned.

There are several morals to this memory: Don't gather a group of people around a pool in an enclosed area and truly believe no one might accidentally fall in. Don't use glass around a pool. Don't skirt around a crowd of people and walk on the very edge of a pool. Don't walk around, or through, or behind a crowd of people with your hands full: More 'Mom' cautions for you.

The last water-related reception memory I have to tell you about was a wedding an assistant shot out on Stout Island, in Wisconsin in 1996. As I have mentioned earlier, as the videographers, we are usually the last to leave the event. The same was true for our assistant at this wedding reception.

Stout Island is exactly that: An island. You park your car on the mainland and get on a ferry which takes you out to the island. Well, at the end of the evening, the ferry was leaving the dock every 30 minutes to bring people back to their cars.

As a videographer, you often tape till the very end especially when hired for the 'Unlimited Package': Videotape until the very end and then catch a shot of the groom carrying the bride over the threshold of the Honeymoon Cabin. With everything done for the night, he packed up his equipment and wheeled down to the docks. As he was approaching the ferry, he met the ferry operator on the pathway, up to the lodge. Upon meeting him, he learned the ferry trips were done for the night; he had missed the last boat for the evening and wouldn't be able to get off the island until 8:00am on Sunday morning.

My assistant mustered up that crazed look that I have perfected so well over the years and explained that he needed to get back to his car and drive back to

"I Do"

Minneapolis that night so he could be at another event the next morning in St. Paul. He needed to get in his car tonight! Even if he didn't have another shoot in St. Paul the following morning, he still had nowhere to stay on the island. The lodge was full and he'd be sleeping on the grass. Whether it was the crazed look or the sad story, we'll never know, but the guy started the boat again.

Can I Get Your Autograph?

Over the years, we have done a lot of weddings for people from all walks of life, including people who fit in the categories of the Minnesota Twins Baseball League, the NFL, the NHL, the NBA, a Hollywood producer, a child of a Hollywood celebrity, and a nephew of a Hollywood/Las Vegas legend along with many people who are either related to someone or are themselves in the local spotlight.

When "I Do" has been hired by people who are celebrities in the world of sports, I am completely oblivious to who's who. Personally, my mind has never been able to grasp the rules and strategies of different games so I have never developed an interest. Well, my first sport celebrity wedding came in May of '92. The groom played for the NFL New Orleans' Saints. When the bride and the mother of the bride came to our house to view our work and sign a contract, we had absolutely no idea there was anything 'out of the norm' about the event. Looking at it in retrospect, the bride told us the groom's name (it had to be on the contract), she told us that he was on television a lot, and she told us where they currently lived and where they were from; no light bulb going off in my world. Hopefully they found the anonymity refreshing and not insulting. I'm going to bet refreshing since they hired us, loved their video and gave us a very nice referral.

Before I get any further into this story, I should tell you my parents are huge football fans. As a matter of fact, my Dad asked my Mom to marry him while they were at the Memorial Coliseum in Los Angeles during the unforgettable (they tell me) 1974 football game between Notre Dame and USC. I have been trained to know that when my parents inform me that football season is upon us, I cannot call them on Monday nights, Thursday nights, Saturday afternoons, or Sunday afternoons. If I do make the mistake of calling (and they actually pick up), it better be an emergency, and it had better be a really, really important emergency!

Well, a month or two before the wedding, I was talking with my Mom on the phone while looking through some upcoming contracts. I was just rambling through the names on the contracts, out loud, and when I got to this particular event, my Mom stopped me. She asked me what the groom's name was, and I told her again. She then asked, "Where do they live?" I said, "Louisiana but they're both originally from St. Paul. Why?" My Mom had obviously recognized the name. She started squealing like an excited baby animal and asked me if she could go to the wedding with me to help carry equipment. I asked who, what, why, where and how, etc. and after she explained everything to me, I think she realized just how much her daughter didn't inherit her football fanaticism. I think I said, "Oh."

The day in May showed up and both my assistant and I shot the wedding (and no, Mom didn't help.) Everything went along just fine and yes, there were several men there who blocked out the sun for all of us other humans who were of average size. The reception was at the International Market Square in Minneapolis. When I arrived with cameras and equipment, I was halted at the door by security and refused entrance into the building. I tried to explain that we were the hired videographers for the day but they just ignored us and attended to other guests entering the building. Eventually the mother of the bride showed up and personally escorted us into the building and we got some great footage. (I should let my Mom see it someday.)

The next two sports related weddings occurred in '95 and '96. Both of these involved people who were a part of the Minnesota Twins Baseball franchise. Once again, I was unaware of who was who in the sports world. At the 1995 wedding, several comments were made during the video interviews about, "Being back from the honeymoon before spring training started," and "Beautiful wedding – We will see you in Florida soon." There were several toasts during dinner, and comments from guests throughout the evening, on video, which included a lot of baseball references. Only after asking my Dad about names and giving him some details did I know what was going on; as usual, completely oblivious.

The second Twins related wedding was in 1996. I was at this wedding with an assistant who was a complete baseball fanatic; the Minnesota Twins, especially.

At the wedding, he didn't say much except look at a lot of people with wide eyes. I figured as long as he did his work, helped me and didn't offend anyone, he could look all he wanted. When we got to the reception at the Edina Country Club, I was finally filled in by my assistant, who gave me a play-by-play of everyone who walked past us; their name and the complete rundown of their stats. I swear the poor boy was going to faint when the owner of the Twins, at that time, walked by. Again, I'm afraid I made a comment similar to, "Neat. Now let's get back to work." I apologize if I didn't pay proper homage; I was just there to do my job.

The next sports-related wedding was also in 1996. The ceremony was in Wisconsin with the reception in Minnesota. Again, it would have helped to not be clueless. Decorations for the wedding were absolutely gorgeous and featured magnificent, floral sprays set six feet up in the air every two pews for the entire length of the church. Since the church did not have a balcony, my back camera was on the main floor at the back of the sanctuary.

Unfortunately, the floral arrangements made it darn close to impossible to get a good shot of anyone doing any reading or singing, but I made it work. The reception went along just fine, too. Towards the end of the night, I was doing some last interviews of guests who decided they wanted to be on camera, after all. During those interviews, I made an out of the blue comment to a guest about how there seemed to be a lot of muscular, beefy-looking guys there who could block out the sun. That's when I found out the groom and a lot of the male guests played hockey for the NHL Washington Capitals.

I have always considered myself a rather tall person. I'm not used to having to crane my neck upward to be able to look into someone's face; just not used to that. However, all that changed when we shot weddings for people who played basketball for the NBA. In 2003, "I Do" was hired for the wedding of a 7' groom who played basketball with the Utah Jazz, and his bride played college-level basketball and was easily 6'5", herself! Imagine being that height! Wow! They definitely won't have short children!

As for the relatives of celebrities, the nephew of the Hollywood/Las Vegas legend had his wedding in Bloomington, MN in the early 1990s; two very nice people who found each other in this great big world, and had a fun wedding day. Anonymity, remember? But to give you a hint about their relative, his initials are A.B. but he worked under the initials of J.B. until someone with the initials of R.H. (who is better known with the initials of B.H.) gave him the new initials of T.B. To quote one of my favorite Saturday Night Live characters, 'Linda Richman' played by Mike Myers, "There's your topic. Now, talk amongst yourselves."

The other celebrity-related wedding was for a pair of college sweethearts. The groom, the son of a Hollywood actor, married a Minnesota girl. His father was the Best Man and the wedding ceremony was put on hold for thirty minutes while the paternal grandmother was en-route from the airport. The hint for identity in this wedding is that the Best man's initials are A.I., but he is best known as T.D. Again, talk amongst yourselves.

Back in the mid-90s, we received a call from a personal assistant of a movie producer, who was conducting 'interviews' for her employer and helping him coordinate his upcoming wedding. While he was producing another movie, his bride-to-be was unable to help much since she was, at the time, residing in London. The groom lived in Minnesota, and the wedding was to take place in Minnesota, as well. We set up a time to visit with her and her employer, and then were given directions to the meeting location.

When we pulled into the parking lot of the meeting location on the day of the appointment, we noticed it was crowded with trailers, catering trucks, and cars. We checked in at the security booth and were directed where to park and which trailer we were to go to for our appointment.

Both he and his assistant were very pleasant people, and he complimented our style of shooting, and our work. However, our documentary style wasn't what he was looking for; he preferred to have his wedding shot in a more 'avant garde' style. For example, he suggested doing something more along the lines of a close up on a dinner plate and following a fork full of food into a guest's mouth and then as they chewed, asking what they thought of the food before they swallowed. He wanted the videographers to be more accessible/'seen' than the unobtrusive, documentary approach taken by videographers with whom he had met with, so far. I asked him if he was looking for more of an 'MTV, Burger King commercial, quick shots with angles, out there and semi-obtrusive style of work.' He confirmed that was exactly what he was looking for and wanted at least 10 videographers in attendance. I politely explained that we were, regrettably, not the videographers for him because of two reasons: The first, we were short-handed for the number of videographers he was looking for, and secondly, to find a professional videographer, with quality work and experience, with the style of filming he was looking for, in the Midwest was going to be nearly impossible. He would be more apt to find that style on the East or West coasts, but definitely not in the Midwest where videography styles were much more conservative in nature – more along the documentary style where the bride and groom are the stars for the day rather than the obnoxious video person. We thanked him for giving us the opportunity to meet with him and his assistant and wished him and his bride-to-be the best of luck.

Their wedding day came and went and through a trusted 'grapevine' of mine, I heard that he wound up hiring a number of camera people who had worked on some of his films. He, in fact, did not hire any local videography companies as I knew he wouldn't. None of us offered him what he was looking for, which is fine. Actually, it was very nice of him to be up front with everyone he met with rather than having many disappointments, after the fact.

As for Elvis, he has been spotted several times at special events and wedding receptions. And as I've heard, he's got quite the business escorting brides down the aisle in Las Vegas!

Calisthenics in Formalwear

Yes, some people are just so excited to get married that they just can't help themselves when it comes to jumping up and down, or bowling, doing cartwheels, or... rolling down hills.

Yes, you read it correctly: Brides and grooms rolling down hills. "I Do" Productions has been fortunate to be hired by incredible people embarking on their lives together. I would have to say the majority of the people we have met have been great whether because of their personalities, their upbeat attitudes, their vivaciousness, or their positive outlook on the world.

The rolling-down-the-hill couple fit all of those qualities. Their ceremony was held at Westminster Presbyterian in downtown Minneapolis. Westminster is already a beautiful church, but the flower arrangements done by Camrose Hill Floral, out of Stillwater, MN made it breathtaking. That wedding took place over 20 years ago and I still remember walking through the large, wooden doors at the back of the sanctuary and being overcome with the most captivating aromas. Before that wedding, I thought flowers were nice and pretty, and that was about it. After I opened those doors, I fell in love with flowers. It was just one of those things where you had to be there. The dark wood, the red carpet and the stained glass all enhanced by the most beautiful floral arrangements you have ever seen across the front of the altar...

Okay, enough of the flowers... I was just having a moment... Apologies... But you should have been there!

Anyway, the reception was held at the Woodhill Country Club in Orono, MN which has a very large hill behind the Clubhouse. During the champagne hour, this vivacious couple each laid down on the ground, she in her gown and he in his tuxedo, and proceeded to roll down the big hill. I'm serious. It's all on video. They got down to the bottom laughing hysterically as their guests, sipping champagne, watched them from the patio above. This is also the reception where when I was standing behind the carving chef to tape the buffet line, he greeted one of the guests by saying, "Good evening, Mrs. (someone who has a line of baking products labeled with her last name.) I feel as if I should go home and bake a cake. There's always time for cake!

At one of the receptions we did at the Medina Ballroom, the bride decided it was time to go bowling at the alley, located inside the building. So, the bride and groom, and a few of their attendants changed their shoes, grabbed some bowling balls, and bowled a game. Of course, with her wedding gown, she managed to set off the foul light on her every turn. By the way, if you were unaware, fouls don't count on your wedding day. Just so you know. I wonder if this rule holds true for traffic/speeding tickets, as well?

One bride, during her pre-ceremony pictures, was so excited she decided to do a cartwheel in the narthex of the church. She was just this big poof of white, for an instant. However, she didn't think about what it might do to her hair or her veil. Her first cartwheel went so well, she decided to do it again and that's when she remembered all of those hours spent doing her hair and getting the veil just right. The pre-ceremony photography was briefly delayed while her hair and veil were restored to their pre-cartwheel perfection.

These remaining stories have no specific relationship to calisthenics. They are simply stories of what people have done while being dressed in formal wear...

Starting from the beginning, if you are planning a large event, please seriously consider valet parking. In 1993, we did a wedding reception out at the Lafayette Club where the couple opted to not provide valet parking. What a mistake! There were at least 500 guests, if not more, and it was just a chaotic, free-for-all parking nightmare, in the dark! My assistant and I shot this wedding and we were lucky enough to arrive just in time to get one of the last parking spots at a small church across the golf course from the Clubhouse. We gathered all of our equipment and joined the other guests in a pilgrimage across the greens to the main building. The moral of this story: Hire valet parking.

After dinner, at this same reception, we were all treated to a ballroom dancing display complete with beautiful hooped-skirt dresses. The bride and groom were fellow members of the group who performed. The Lafayette Club provided an ideal backdrop for this lovely performance as we videotaped from the balcony.

While most couples are not part of a Ballroom Dancing Troupe, many will take professional dance lessons prior to their big day so they are able to do something more than what I refer to as the 'washing machine dance.' You've seen this dance... Where the couple rock back and forth and spin around in circles, slowly, reminding you of the agitation cycle of a washing machine, hence the name. For the people who take dance lessons, their efforts usually pay off well from what they learned in class, plus the rest of the time they are on the dance floor, they look like they are having more fun because they know what they are doing.

There have been couples who have hired swing bands for their receptions. The group can play other music, too, but specialize in swing and will also teach the crowd how to do a couple of moves. The basic instruction reminds me of aerobic classes and pretty soon everyone has the order of the moves down pat. The tricky part comes when the music is added and the moves are to a beat; then it all goes down the drain and usually dissolves into laughter.

I have found that people in the 'north country' love to polka. 'Roll Out the Barrel' will start and everyone who was just on the edge of a deep sleep at their table suddenly jumps up from their chair, shrieks, and runs out onto the dance floor as if their backsides were on fire. They find the nearest single person, who is also shrieking their way onto the dance floor, clasp them around the waist and then they start swirling each other around as fast as possible. This dance is nothing more than a 'Tilt-a-Whirl' ride at the fair! The trick is to not run into any other couples while spinning (though it probably adds to the fun), and to definitely not tangle your feet with your partner's feet and find yourself sitting on the floor.

Once at the FantaSuites Hotel in Burnsville, MN (cool place, by the way) the mother of the bride and the aunt of the bride were doing the polka and fell over, right in front of the DJ's set up. They were both laughing hysterically and were helped up by the other guests, but the aunt was so dizzy, she fell against the DJ's stand and slumped back onto the floor. She sat there a little bit to get her bearings before she attempted to stand up again.

Another sitting-rather-than-dancing situation was in Minneapolis, in '95. The bride and groom were successfully doing the polka until the groom stepped on the hem of the bride's dress. The bride hit the floor and the groom fell on top of her. The couple following them in the circle, from behind, was unaware of the sudden roadblock, and tripped over the newlyweds. Four people were now on the floor. People began helping these four off the dance floor, and that's when the fun really began. One woman was pulled up and was busy straightening her dress when the man on the floor decided to use her leg as a grip to pull himself up. She fell back on the floor and took down another woman who tried to save her as she fell backward. The man got up to help the (now two) women and the laughing newlyweds off the dance floor. One woman up; groom up; and finally the second woman was vertical; she quickly removed herself from the dance floor so she wouldn't fall again. But it wasn't over. As the bride was being helped by the groom, the first woman began to walk away but the heel of her shoe was caught on the bride's gown which caused her to again start falling. She grabbed the nearest person who happened to be the groom who was helping up the bride and all three of them hit the floor again. Eventually, everyone got off the floor, but it definitely took a while.

At this same wedding, my assistant was standing on a chair videotaping the 'Hokey Pokey' [code for: Preliminary Inebriation/Alcoholic Test (PIT/PAT)]. After the dance was done, my assistant was waiting for the crowd to clear before he got down off the chair. As he was about to get down, I saw a guy coming towards him with his arm extended but I was sure he would pull his arm in at the last moment, but he didn't... He 'clothes-lined' my assistant's legs causing him to lose his balance while holding the video camera and teeter over the shoulder of this guy. After a split second, my assistant toppled over the back of him and landed on the dance floor.

I ran over to where my assistant was forced into doing unexpected acrobatics. I got to the dance floor just as he landed and before I could say anything, the man said, "Oh, don't be worried. He'll be okay." I, without hesitation said, "I'm not worried about him! It's the camera I'm worried about!" The guy laughed and my assistant, feeling truly cared about, handed me the camera, and made his way off the dance floor.

On the subject of people on the shoulders of other people, in the late 90s, I shot a wedding in a small farming community in northern Minnesota. This is one of those towns where everyone else knows everyone else's business – and if they don't, they'll simply fill in the blanks and get a new rumor started which will burn through town like wildfire. This particular town also has an unwritten rule about any wedding receptions which may be held in the town's city hall ballroom, above the liquor store and restaurant. At 8:00pm, unless otherwise requested and noted, the general public is welcome to join the party for their Friday or Saturday evening 'scheduled' entertainment.

Back to my small town story: The father of the bride was very prominent within the community and knew just about everyone and if not, rest assured, everyone knew him. The wedding was perfect, and the reception dinner was grand. But then, sure enough, around 8:00pm the crowd swelled as the first dance began. People who weren't officially invited wanted to either see who was there, pretend to be part of the invited guest list, or just jaw-wag with some of the guests who received an official invitation. Around 9:30pm, it had somewhat thinned, but there was still a substantial crowd. The DJ announced the next song was dedicated to the groom by some of his friends. I held the camera up and was ready to film when one of the groomsmen came over to me and warned me that I should stay off the dance floor; it was a better idea if I were up on the riser with the DJ. I heeded his warning and stood next to the DJ.

An alternative rock song came on and all the guys on the dance floor, including the groom, started 'slam dancing.' I had already seen 'dancing' like this at receptions in the Twin Cities so it didn't faze me, but you should have seen the looks on the faces of the older folks in this small town. After a minute or two of belly-bucking, the guys hoisted the groom up over their heads and he started body surfing on his friends. I don't believe one person was talking in that entire ballroom. All eyes were on the performance of the new son-in-law and his 'interesting' friends. Personally, I thought it looked like a lot of fun!

There is something that brides, their bridesmaids and flower girls like to do. This particular activity is actually learned when they are little girls and it secretly follows them through their lives. It's called 'twirling.' The great thing about twirling is that you can do it anywhere as long as you have a dress or skirt that will properly 'poof' out. It's sort of a Cinderella thing. I have hours of footage of brides, bridesmaids, flower girls, moms, grandmothers, and guests twirling. This will first happen when they first try on the dress at the store if the 'poof factor' is desired. It will happen again when they put on the dress for their wedding. It will happen when they see their groom for the first time or anyone else for that matter because they will be asked to turn around and show off their dress. It happens during the photography and it happens a lot at the reception with all the dancing and spinning. Basically, twirling... Twirling can happen anywhere and it makes you happy.

Speaking of twirling, in 1992, I shot a reception in Stillwater where the bride couldn't have been any taller than five feet and didn't weigh anything more than 100 pounds. She was just tiny. Anyway, the specialty dance of 'I Knew The Bride When She Used To Rock-n-Roll' came on and everyone formed a circle around her and began to take turns dancing with her in the center. One of the participants who wanted to dance with her was a male relative who had to have been at least 6'5" and weight 275 pounds. When it was his turn, he bounded into the center and since he towered over the bride by a good foot and a half, he picked her up by the waist and began to twirl her around. She held onto his neck for dear life as her body flew out horizontally from its center point (him), and the circle of people widened so no one would get kicked in the face by her flailing feet. People were clapping and cheering him on and he just kept spinning her faster. Nearly after 30 rotations, he slowed down and eventually set her back down on the dance floor. She instantly fell down. She tried a couple of times to get back up with the help of the guests but just couldn't get her bearings. Her husband then came over and picked her up off the dance floor and set her on a nearby chair so the dancing could continue and she wouldn't get stepped on. Her relative is one guy you wouldn't want on your dance card. Or, maybe you would...

Each culture has it's different traditional dances. At Greek, Russian, and Jewish weddings we have seen people crouch into a sitting position and kick their legs out in a rapid, alternating succession; some fall and some don't. As for me, I would barely be able to get into that crouching position let alone have my brain grasp the idea of purposely kicking my legs out from under me. For another dance, some people cross their arms and hold onto their partner's forearms and spin as fast as they can and then try to not fall over when finished.

At Jewish weddings, the newlyweds and guests partake in a circular dance called the 'Hora' where they lift people up on chairs, in the center. Of all the Horas I have ever seen, everything has gone along just fine, even for the people who might be a bit heavier than the norm when they are lifted. However, there was one reception where the men lifted the mother of the groom (who was not overweight) but managed to drop her. She fractured her wrist when she hit the floor. Although she was embarrassed and upset, she handled the situation with grace.

The Polish, and some African cultures, incorporate a broom into their celebrations. Whether the broom is at the ceremony or the reception, the couple is expected to jump over the broom together. Most often the broom is placed on the floor and a little hop over it takes care of the tradition. At a reception in Stillwater, two people held the broom off the floor a few inches which turned out to be a big mistake. The bride's shoe caught the handle which made her trip. Fortunately, she was caught by the groom who was holding her arm.

Speaking of tumbling brides, there have been two incidents involving staircases and one involving an escalator. The first couple was descending the grand, curved staircase at the Calhoun Beach Club in Minneapolis as they were announced to their reception guests. Halfway down, the bride's heel caught the previous stair's tread and she started to tumble. Her knight in shining armor - or black tuxedo, if you prefer – was holding onto her arm and kept her from tumbling all the way down.

The second bride was also descending a staircase with her groom at the Plymouth Radisson. But it was the groom who committed the faux pas – he stepped on the hem of her dress which caused her to start tumbling. Fortunately, he was there for the save and everyone cheered.

The third bride was coming down an escalator with her bridal party as part of the grand march into an atrium at a St. Paul venue where dinner was being served. The bride and the groom were the last couple down the escalator, and just as she was about to glide off effortlessly, she found that her shoe's spiky heel was caught between the metal grooves of the step. Before she got to the bottom, she sort of hopped around on the step while holding onto her groom's arm. At the bottom she walked off and turned around to witness her shoe being pressed into the metal grate at the bottom of the escalator. Finally, the heel snapped off the shoe and both pieces were released. Needless to say, it wasn't exactly the graceful entrance she envisioned. She then walked to the head table, bobbing up and down all the way; one shoe on, one shoe off.

I will end this section with the frivolities surrounding the bouquet tosses and garter removals. For the most part, bouquet tosses go well. Some brides are spun around several times until they get dizzy and then, hopefully, the only thing they toss is their bouquet. If they manage to toss their bouquet without having it disintegrate against the ceiling, a chandelier, or a ceiling fan, the female guests will generally tear at each other to catch the flowers. Some guests will even scramble around on the floor to grab the prize of the now hacked-on bouquet. Strange...

As for garter removals, I think the funniest one I have ever seen was at the Minnesota History Center in '94. When the groom finally stopped dancing around and got over to the bride, he knelt down and covered himself with the skirt of the bride's gown. The first item he pulled out was a racquetball racket, quickly followed by a pair of handcuffs, then a can of pop, followed by a pair of huge men's underwear. Finally, he pulled off the garter and got on with the toss to the male guests. The whole thing was very funny and, to this day, I still wonder where all that stuff was hiding before she sat down?

What's on the Menu?

Along with flowers, because of weddings, I like food. In fact, it's not so much the food, as it is, the 'presentation' of the meal. Since I have four kids and a busy lifestyle, the majority of our family meals consist of Monday night meatloaf, and Thursday night spaghetti, over and over each week. But since I incorporated the line about being provided a meal into "I Do's" contract, we fortunately get a reprieve from Tuesday night tacos with every reception we do.

I have seen some beautiful meals. And the taste? To die for! Once for dinner at the Lafayette Country Club on Lake Minnetonka, I was served a bacon-wrapped filet mignon which was placed on fresh asparagus and then topped with a waffle-cut potato slice, a curl of tomato and a curl of carrot, with a sprig of parsley. The Béarnaise sauce for the asparagus was artistically drizzled on the perimeter of the plate. It was so beautiful, I videotaped it. Oh, by the way, very delicious! Très bien! (I took four years of high school French so, I can say that.)

I have been treated to watermelon soup at a hotel in Bloomington, and enjoyed Bananas Foster at Windows on Minnesota (before it became an insurance 'no-no' because of the open flame.) I've also had strawberry soup but, for the life of me, cannot remember where. It was scrumptious, though.

Some receptions have been designed with multiple food stations set up so guests could choose from various cuisines such as Italian, Oriental and American. Another nice touch, regardless of how dinner was served, are the dessert tables featuring the wedding cake. The tables are usually filled with fruit filled tortes, petits fours, fresh fruit kabobs with chocolate fondue, cream-filled cakes, cookies, candies, a variety of mousses and the now ever-popular chocolate fountains. (Yes, I have a 'sweet tooth.' I've found heaven!) The coffee bars are quite a treat, as well! There are a variety of different coffees served in the silver urns with the claw feet and the bowls of chocolate shavings, cinnamon sticks and sugar cubes served in crystal bowls atop white linens. Once again, it's all in the presentation. I have assured my children that their weddings will all have dessert tables and coffee bars, without fail.

A handful of our receptions have served filet mignon and lobster tail, and I had the best 'Chicken a la Oscar' at the Town and Country Club in St. Paul. I know that to some of you, these dishes may not sound like a big deal but, to us, they are fabulous! I have always said, "The best things I make in the kitchen are reservations to go elsewhere." But now, since we have children, I rarely get to make reservations anymore and am relegated to eating a lot of peanut butter and jelly sandwiches.

We have all been to some other weddings, however, where we have been served dishes that are definitely different from our weekly fare. At one Oriental wedding reception, my assistant was treated to duck feet during his seven course meal. Yes, duck feet. Those morsels were included in one of the entrees served, and among the people who were seated with my assistant, he was the only daring soul to try the delicacy. As he stated, "Once the duck's feet were cooked, I felt it was too late to give them back."

A particular Chinese wedding reception, which stands out in my memory, would be one from St. Paul a few years ago. The couple, with their families, hosted a 10-course meal of authentic Chinese foods. When I spoke with them prior to the wedding to confirm all of their information, they all assured me that I should come to the reception with a big appetite and be ready to eat. As I mentioned earlier, I love food and Chinese cuisine is definitely one of my favorites.

The first course consisted of a soup. So far, so good. I though the soup was delicious and while still eating asked one of the teenagers sitting at my table, "What kind of soup is this? What's in it?" She told me it was 'Maw' soup. I pursued the point, "What is maw?" and she replied, "Fish intestines." Though I had thought it was good, that answer pretty much ended course one for me. From the look on my face, the people at my table all picked up on the fact that they were going to be greatly entertained by my introduction to *authentic* Chinese cuisine.

My children have taught me the 'verbiage,' but I refrained from saying the words "yucky" or "gross." I sat quietly at the table, with visions of cheeseburgers dancing through my head and attended to the videotaping of any toasts, or other activities up at the head table. Another course involved sushi. My foreign cuisine adventures come to a screeching halt when sushi is served. I just can't go there.

While everyone else at my table was enjoying their food, I was trying to figure out what the different items were. There was an unidentifiable piece of meat (?) that was shiny, wet, black and discus-shaped with a diameter of one or two inches. And if that doesn't make your imagination run wild, it also had a brilliant turquoise, thin inner-ring. The teens at the table thought it was perhaps a type of eel. Actually, it was very pretty – but very disturbing, at the same time. If you are reading this paragraph and know what I'm talking about, please let me know – I've been wondering about this for over a decade, now.

Later in the evening, the photographer and I were leaving at the same time. As we were packing up our equipment, I said, "I really do like Chinese food but the meal tonight was a bit much. Did you eat any of the food?" He nodded with an unsatisfied look on his face and said, "I had to. I was sitting with some of the family members and I didn't want to appear rude and refuse to eat, how about you?" I replied, "After the soup course, I was done. By the way, do you know what that black and turquoise cut of sushi was?" "I have absolutely no idea and I'm so hungry," he said. I informed him about the McDonald's right down the road as we walked out the door. Both of us were in the fast food drive-thru within minutes.

As much as it may sound like I am squeamish when it comes to trying new foods, I really am not. I know I wouldn't go to the extent of what the 'Survivor' reality show makes the contestants eat, but I do try to keep an open mind when something new is placed before me. As a matter of fact, I did a Scottish wedding a number of years ago, complete with bagpipers and kilts. At the reception dinner, the offer of haggis was made. The haggis was placed on a large silver platter surround by kale, and wheeled into the ballroom. The bride and groom introduced the Scottish dish and described to us its ingredients and how it was prepared. Haggis, for those of you who don't know, consists of a sheep's liver, heart and lungs along with oatmeal and various spices combined and stuffed into a sheep's stomach bag during the baking process. Being adventurous, I joined the other guests in line to receive a serving of haggis. It wasn't bad.

I also enjoy the cuisine served at Eastern Indian wedding receptions. I have been to several, and the food, as you might imagine, is hot – very hot. My assistant made the mistake of picking up a chip, about the size of a Dorito chip, and popped the entire thing into his mouth, chewed and swallowed it. After a moment or two, he figured out why the other guests sitting at the table were watching him so intently while he was eating. The heat showed up. He needed water. A lot of it, and fast!

The guests who were watching him were now laughing at him. He then understood why there were only 10 chips in a basket per table.

Of course, if you don't want to be daring and try haggis, spicy chips, or sushi, you can always go with chicken. Did you know there are close to 1,000 ways to prepare and serve chicken? Seriously. It became a joke for when all of us would talk about the various weddings, receptions, and event happenings, including what was served for dinner. For example, one assistant would say, "I had chicken #348 (Chicken Cordon Bleu) and you?" I would reply, "#782 (chicken with a cream sauce served on rice pilaf.)" Seriously though, the meals are usually great and a big step up from our weekly Wednesday night macaroni and cheese nights, with the kids.

Feeling Hot, Hot, Hot...

On August 7, 1998, I was at a reception held at a popular lodge/resort property in the Brainerd, MN lakes area. When I arrived at the reception, I stashed all of my extra equipment into the coat closet next to the front door and began videotaping. After the dinner had been finished and the guests were beginning to eat their cake, the best man decided it was the perfect time to offer his toast. Just as he began, one of the bridesmaids screamed "FIRE!" People, at first, looked around confused and then the word 'FIRE' was shouted again and people started noticing smoke pouring out of the ventilation system. The reception hall was on fire! There were three sets of sliding glass doors near the table where I was sitting and the guests started rushing toward these doors. I could have joined the masses and ran out of one of these doors however my equipment was in the coat closet on the other side of the building. With my camera and tripod in hand, I started bucking against the crowd in order to get where I needed to go. People were shouting, "You're going the wrong way! You need to turn around!" I shouted back, "No! My equipment is that way! The ceremony tapes are that way!" I made it to the coat closet, picked up my equipment and ran out the front door.

I was one of the last people out of the building. While everyone was corralled out on the lawn, down by the lake, the fire department delivered the news that the laundry room, in the basement, caught on fire because some linens in the dryer became too hot. When the fire was out, everyone was allowed back into the building and the reception continued as if nothing had happened. I will state our motto now: "No matter rain, tornado, scorching heat, snow, blizzard, mosquitoes and other bugs, or running through a building on fire, "I Do" Productions has been dedicated to their clients." I just needed to say that... Thank you.

People should think twice about combining silk flowers or dried floral arrangements with candles. It's just a fire hazard waiting to happen. There have been a handful of weddings over the years where candles in candelabras, decorated with silk ivy garlands, were lit too early prior to the ceremony. Before the ceremony is finished, the candles have burned down to the garlands which have started them to either smoke, or catch on fire completely. Two times, there have been these types of fires: One was put out by a fire-extinguisher, and the other was put out by a groomsman who doused the fire with the water from a floral arrangement sitting on the altar.

"I Do"

This same fire hazard warning applies to receptions, too. Usually, it's the votive candles or the floating candles mingled in flowers will catch fire and even fresh flowers and greens will smoke. At one wedding, a few years ago, the dried floral arrangement caught fire on the table where I was sitting. The fire then leapt to a nearby paper napkin a guest had by their drink. This person, thankfully, had the intelligence to not throw their alcoholic beverage on the fire but instead put it out with a carafe of water. An alcohol enhanced fire would definitely have been a mess!

Call "911!"

With all of my pregnancies, you'd think it could have been me who went into labor at one of the weddings where I was videotaping. Actually, it was another woman, still two weeks from her due date, who got up from the dinner table when her water broke. I was adjusting the camera and getting ready to videotape the first dance when I noticed people suddenly standing up and then a frantic voice calling out, "Call 911! She's having a baby!" The paramedics showed up rather quickly and remedied the situation... And the reception didn't turn into a 'birth'day party!

Another '911' call happened about 5 minutes after the father of the groom stood up and made his toast. Apparently, he was on a medication that was not supposed to be combined with alcoholic beverages. He had just a sip of champagne and then stood up to give his toast. At its conclusion, he raised his glass to the couple and then, being caught up in the moment, drank all the rest of the champagne. As other toasts were in progress, the groom's father abruptly leaned against his wife, his chair slid on the marble floor out from underneath him, and he fell to the floor.   The toasts came to a sudden halt as panic struck.

Paramedics were called immediately and he was taken to the hospital. Some guests came back to the reception and were happy to announce that he was just fine... He had accidentally made a little mistake with his toast when he drank the champagne.

Lastly, if you ever see someone meandering out the door to get into their car while drunk, PLEASE take their keys away!!!! Attack them, if necessary!!! Throw them on the ground; pummel them to separate their hand from the car keys!!!!!

I say this because I have heard, post-reception, of several instances where people have gone out to their cars to drive home because they are tired and are "perfectly fine," only to have an accident in the parking lot, drive the wrong way down a street of oncoming traffic, including two separate occasions where the inebriated person entered an off-ramp when they would have normally gotten onto the on ramp: One was on a straight away and able to pull over onto the side before having an accident. The other one wasn't so lucky when looping around on the cloverleaf and had a head-on accident with a car exiting the freeway.   I personally saw this accident as I was getting into my car that night. Not good.

One father of the groom, while leaving the parking lot, became frustrated when he couldn't find the exit in the dark. Of course, it would have helped to have his headlights on... After running his car into a few of the other cars out in the lot, he backed his car up over the curb and straight into a pond about 20 feet from the parking lot. Someone should have definitely grabbed his keys before he left the reception!

Wedding Day Tensions

Every wedding involves some amount of tension during the planning process and on the wedding day itself. Thankfully, most of these stress points are either eliminated or are set aside during the wedding day and resolved at a later time. However, some people will not wait for a later date and continue to voice/display their feelings on the day of the wedding, be it theirs, or someone else's special day.

Back in 1990, I signed a couple for a June of '91 wedding. The bride and her mom came to our house for an appointment, were impressed with our work, and signed a contract. While they were at our house, they also talked about other facets of the planning process and what types of difficulties they were experiencing, especially since the bride lived in Atlanta at the time. On the way out the door, the bride's mom looked over her shoulder and with a laugh said, "By the time this wedding is over, my husband and I will be divorced!" Well, I didn't think too much of her comment because my Mom had said practically the same thing (due to stress) when we were planning my wedding, and my parents remain married to this day.

When the wedding day arrived, everything went along just fine and I really didn't notice a problem between the bride's parents; they weren't 'cuddly-smoochy' but they weren't running each other over with cars in the parking lot, either.

I had found the bride's mom for the parent interview segment of my taping (best wishes, congratulations, stories on videotape to the couple, etc.) but still had to locate the bride's father. I was just about to give up the search when I looked over at the bar, and saw him there, hunched over. I tapped him on the shoulder, introduced myself, and asked him if he would like to join his wife for the parent interview out in the lobby. While he kept his left elbow on the bar, presumably to keep his balance, he swiveled his body around to face me and with his drink in his left hand and a cigar in his right, he firmly stated, "I wouldn't stand or sit near that ^&^*^%&^$%$@@% *&^%$#$% (are you getting creative?) *&^#$%!@%% *&$%%@@#))@@! If you paid me all the money in the world!"

I left the bar and found the mom of the bride to tell her that more than likely, her husband would not be joining her on the video. She had been right, they would be divorced. From that day on, I have always asked about, and included, the marital status of all parents and grandparents on all the contracts we have ever made.

"I Do"

Of course there are also the divorced parents who bring their new 'significant others' to the wedding. I have seen drinks 'accidentally' spilled on another person, creative name-calling spats, and looks that would send chills up most people's spines.

We have also had a handful of mother-in-laws who don't approve (for whatever reason) to the marriages and have had no problems sharing their viewpoint with anyone who will listen on the wedding day. I had one mother of the groom tell me, "I will not say anything on video to my son and that whore he married!" Okey-dokey and alrighty, then! I'm going to go over here, now...

There was another mother of a groom who wore a black dress with a black veil covering her face during the wedding ceremony. You can really tell she was looking forward to that marriage.

Speaking of Moms, in 1996, I was busy videotaping a reception when the mother of the bride came up to me and said she had something important to say to me. With a smile, I said, "Sure." She looked at me with the most terse and threatening look she could muster, waggled her bony finger in my face, moved closer to me and with her New York City 'mafia' accent said, "If you lose any of the pictures that I sent to you for my daughter's and son-in-law's photo montage, I will hunt you down and make you disappear!" I was pleased and relieved to say, "The photo montage is done and all of the photos have already been returned to the couple." After she heard my answer, she backed off and walked away. I apparently had foiled her opportunity to order a mob hit.

The last tension filled evening I will share with you was from a wedding during the month of September 1994. Again, everything was just fine until someone ran into the reception hall from the parking lot and shouted "FIGHT! In the parking lot!" Like a typical bar crowd, everyone pushed their way out of the front door to find it was the bride and groom going at it, in the parking lot. There was more name calling than anything but, they were definitely fighting. There are many unfortunate details to this situation. I don't know what specifically sparked the fight, but I do know they had started drinking alcohol around noon before their ceremony had even begun. I know they went 'bar-hopping' on the way to the reception. And I know there was more drinking at the reception with the open bar. To this day, I don't know if they are still married, but I would have to bet, "No."

Mr. & Mrs. Microphone

The word 'microphone,' when spoken, can cause many types of reactions in many types of people. Some people are great, for example a great singer with an incredible band. Some people shudder with fear and run for the nearest bathroom – they sure are surprised, though, when we follow them. Just kidding! We wait outside – they'll have to come out of there at some point, and then we pounce. I'm kidding, again. Some people, however, should never come near a microphone...

I will first start this chapter off with a few stories of people who are great with microphones. As I mentioned in the previous paragraph: Bands and great singers. The Minneapolis/St. Paul area has an amazing array of immeasurable talent when it comes to this subject. In retrospect, I should have hired a band for my wedding rather than our lousy DJ (more on him later.) Other people who are great on the microphone are relatives, especially grandparents, who give a personal message on the videotape. Even though they appear nervous and may not want to speak on camera, some of their comments, stories and well-wishes are just the best things I've ever heard during my lifetime. And as you can tell from this book, I have seen and heard a lot, over the years.

Of course, I should also say it is helpful when the grandparents remember the names of the bride and groom when addressing them on their video. There have been a few times when the grandparents will sit down, take the microphone and say, "Laurie and Jim, congratulations! Grandpa and I were reminiscing about our wedding day at your ceremony this afternoon and Laurie, you looked so beautiful up there on the altar, and Jim was so handsome..." And then there is a pause and some whispering off camera, then she will continue with, "What? Oh, I'm sorry! Joe was so handsome... Didn't I say Joe? Oops!" she would say with a little chuckle. "As I was saying, dears...."

Bridal party toasts during dinner, as long as it is done in good taste in an appropriate amount of time, can be acceptable when it comes to being on a microphone. The other two who are great on a microphone, naturally, are when the bride and groom whisper sweet nothings to each other up on the altar. Those sincere, little comments are what make a great video.

And that's a 'wrap' describing the few instances which are 'it' for ideal situations and people on microphones. Here are all of the rest of the memories involving microphones and people:

"I Do"

The bride, who is escorted up to the altar by her father, takes her groom's arm and says, "Man! I can't wait to get out of this damn dress and have a beer! How long do you think this ceremony is going to take?" Apparently, she forgot the groom had a wireless microphone on his lapel which transmits a clear signal right onto their videotape.

"I Do" has also had a handful of couples who run a fashion and gossip commentary between each other during communions. Most of it is simply recognizing who came to the ceremony and maybe a nice comment on the color of a guest's dress. One such couple, however, took it a step further in Stillwater. The groom didn't have much to say – he just nodded his head a lot. But the bride was a chatterbox. I remember such comments from her as, "Who invited them?", "Oh, my gosh! Look at that dress she is wearing! I wouldn't be caught dead in that thing!", "Did they get back together?", and "See that old lady right there? She's my great-aunt, and she is an absolute witch!" This was a wedding I shot, and I was sitting up in the balcony doing my best not to laugh out loud – not only at some of the comments, but at the obvious fact the bride was unaware I could hear her whispers, clear as a bell from 300 feet away – and it was all being recorded. Fortunately, I had two other audio sources to cover over her opinions, and another camera view from the front to catch their guests as they came through the communion line.

Grooms, who don't listen to our instructions to not touch the transmitter, etc., because they 'know what they are doing' when it comes to their vast knowledge about lapel microphones, are usually the ones who sabotage the audio on their own wedding videos. I, personally, have had three weddings where the groom 'knows all about microphones' and wound up with not-so-good audio.

One groom didn't listen to me when I told him not to touch the transmitter, and that it was already on. Right before he walked down the aisle with his parents, I saw him from the front camera's view, reach into his jacket and then my audio feed for him went dead. He then put a big smile on his face and marched down the aisle with his parents. I was stuck, up in the balcony by myself, operating the remote for the front camera during the processional. Unless by some miracle, I got his attention from 150 feet away, or he decided to turn his microphone back on, there was going to be no direct audio for the vows and rings. The front camera was about 12 feet away from the couple; I would have audio on that camera, but it was going to be faint. I also had another audio feed from the church's audio system which had the pastor's microphone, so I figured I was going to be okay. When it came to the vows, though, the pastor stood on the top step while the couple remained on the floor – they didn't move up onto the next step. I heard the vows off the pastor's microphone from six feet away, and that was the best it was going to get. During the editing process, the audio signal was boosted during the vows and rings but it would have sounded so much better if the groom would have just listened to me and not touched the microphone.

After the ceremony, while they were organizing the receiving line, I rushed up to the groom and said, "I need your microphone for a second." He pulled the transmitter out of his coat pocket and asked, "Don't I wear this during the receiving line, too?" I said, "Yes, and it's helpful when it's turned on and transmitting, too." The bride overheard this and looked at her new husband with a troubled look. I then quickly explained to both of them how the groom turned off the transmitter off right before he walked down the aisle. They were grateful for what they got but it would have helped if he hadn't messed with it.

The second groom thought the lapel clip, which was already hidden by the boutonnière, was going to be seen by the photographer during the ceremony, from 200 feet away. Keep in mind, the clip is smaller than your pinky fingernail, is black, and is also hiding behind a giant orchid boutonnière. Sure, I could see his reasoning (I'm being sarcastic here.) In his infinite wisdom, he unclipped the microphone from his lapel and shoved it into his pants pocket. How was anyone going to hear the vows and rings and anything else from inside his pants pocket? I was in the balcony messing with the receiver during the entire ceremony thinking something was wrong on my end. I thankfully, again, had the front camera and the direct audio from the church's audio system. When I approached the couple afterwards, I told them I had a bit of difficulty getting any audio on the receiver and I couldn't figure out why since it worked perfectly before the ceremony. Then I pulled the transmitter off the back waistband of his pants, and instead of following the wire up over his shoulder and onto the lapel of his coat, I had found what he had done. I asked him why he had done that, and that's when he told both me and his now very unhappy bride about his not-so-wise decision. At least that explained the problem I was having and saved me an unnecessary bill to get my microphone 'fixed'... They are even more expensive to replace.

The third incredibly smart groom decided he would keep his transmitter on when he needed to speak and then turn it off when he wasn't speaking. The editing process was difficult, to say the least. Besides having both camera views synchronized, we also sync the three audio sources. Well, with this wedding, the most important audio source (the groom) was not a steady signal. Although it wasn't easy, we managed to get the audio lined up with the video (this was before non-linear editing making it very difficult) so it wouldn't look like an old movie where someone's mouth moves, and then later you hear their audio.

I am reminded of one other story regarding the switching on and off of the microphone but it wasn't the groom, it was the priest. This was back in '96, out in White Bear Lake. The priest was an elderly fellow and the situation was just cute and terribly funny. Typically, officiants will reach under their robes and turn off the transmitter when they aren't using it throughout the entire service or ceremony. This priest was a bit confused and had this process backwards. He would turn the microphone off when he got up to talk or sing, and then turn it back on when he was done. No one could hear him very well when he was talking during the Gospel or the homily, but the entire congregation could hear him, clear as a bell, talking to himself when he was looking through the Bible, and when he was prepping the Communion on the altar and other various times throughout the ceremony. It was a very amusing service.

While we are on the discussion of ceremony locations, there is one church in northeast Minneapolis which I shot at about a decade ago. It was a Friday night wedding, and apparently the Minneapolis Police Department was out in full force that evening, in patrol cars. Every so often, throughout the entire ceremony, our wireless microphone receiver would pick up radio transmissions of squad cars driving by. Again, the second camera's audio saved the day, and no patrol cars drove by during the vows and rings. This is the only church any of our crews have ever experienced this particular problem. Another problem location, though, is a church in Roseville, MN, right across the highway from some very tall radio towers. The transmission from those towers is so strong, it is nearly impossible to have any wireless microphone transmit, at a 100% performance, in that church.

Receiving lines have one comment frequently transmitted onto videotape. The grooms will still have the wireless lapel microphone on for the receiving line – it's sort of the 'sneaky' way to get guest interviews. Anyway, we have heard this question (in multiple variations) between the bride and groom during the receiving line: The groom will lean over and whisper to the bride, "Who are these people coming up next?" She'll whisper back, "I'm not sure, just pretend you know." He will acknowledge with, "Okay. I hope they brought a nice gift."

Groomsmen will also provide much humor when they find out the groom has been 'wired up.' 95% of them will pretend they, too, have a lapel microphone on and that they are involved in a secret spy mission while holding up their lapel and speaking into it using code words and phrases. Or they immediately run over to the groom's lapel and shout, "Check, check, 1, 2, 3, check!" Or the favorite buzz phrase of this time, "Can you hear me now?" Five to ten minutes after I have wired-up the groom, I'll get up to the balcony to check on the signal strength and if I have still have transmission or not, and if I do, the guys will still be talking about the microphone and goofing around in the middle of a 'spy mission.' On the package containing the microphone, it should be written, 'Not only is it essential for the ceremony audio but it provides a lot of entertainment for the groom and his groomsmen.' Boys and their toys...

We are all familiar with the campaign, 'Don't drink and drive.' Well, there should also be a rule of, 'Don't drink and pick up a microphone.' Somewhere in the early 90s, the option of singing a song with the word 'LOVE' in it to get the bride and groom to kiss, during dinner, became an alternative to clinking glasses. 'L-O-V-E' by Nat King Cole is, of course, the perfect song for this activity. Others we have heard include the theme from the Love Boat TV series, the jingle from Oscar Mayer Weiner, and the Biblical 'Jesus Loves Me' which is always adorable when a child sings the song. Let's not forget the theme song from the children's show, 'Barney,' "I love you, you love me, we're a happy family..."

There are many, many songs out there to fit this option and there are many, many types of singers who sing these songs. A lot of people will stand up together to hide their individual voices, or there are the people who have no fear of getting up and singing by themselves because they have great voices, but then there is that group of people who feel their voices and talent improve when alcohol is involved. This latter group also has no idea as to what they are doing; open bars during the champagne/cocktail hour will usually provide the most entertainment during dinner. I have seen people stand up on their chairs to serenade the couple then fall off of them as they are trying to get back down. One guy who wanted even more height, stepped from the seat of his chair onto the table, but accidentally stepped in his salad plate. I have seen a person sit on the edge of the head table and sing to a dismayed couple. Drunk and tone deaf is not a preferred combination.

Take the melody out of the mix and now we have the toasts. My assistant had one groomsman who literally took 52 minutes for his best man toast. According to the itinerary for the day (which obviously was not shared with this individual), the best man's toast would be first, followed by a champagne toast, and then dinner would be served. At first, the couple though it was funny, as did everyone else listening, when he continued past a natural break point. After 10 minutes though, the bride's face took on a tolerant look and the groom followed suit. At 15 minutes, the bride and groom became downright perturbed. They delicately tried to get the best man to end all of his stories, and thoughts, but to no avail... He just kept going.

During his never ending speech, the Catering Director mentioned to the mother of the bride that the food was ready to be served and if this toast didn't end soon, the food would be served cold. After the Mom made hand gestures signaling the dinner service towards the very unhappy bride, a nod was given and the executive decision was made to deviate from the itinerary and get on with the show. The best man wrapped up his toast when he noticed everyone else had finished eating and ended with the line, "Well, I suppose I should sit down and eat now." This last line was followed by a round of applause, not necessarily because of what he had to say but, simply, because he was finished speaking. The champagne toast was given during the cake service, and I don't think he will ever be asked to be the best man again.

There is one other best man which I will mention. This reception was at the Minneapolis Golf Club and thankfully he didn't speak for 52 minutes! He was funny guy and gave a good speech. For a wrap up, he did a 'David Letterman Top 10 List' in regards to the wedding, complete with the snare drum intro. The last line of his toast was, "And the #1 reason for Holly's and Dave's wedding? Because Holly's Mom and Dad had nothing better do with $35,000!" It was absolutely hilarious! And even though he went beyond the standard 3 to 5 minute toast, he kept everyone in stitches.

A decade ago at the St. Paul Hotel, the bridal party during dinner, individually wished the couple well and then altogether 'toasted' the couple; literally. Each person had a piece of toasted bread and on the count of 'three' tossed their toast at the couple. This is the only time I've seen this and I thought it was very clever.

There is also one other alternative option for getting the bride and groom to kiss during dinner, which we have seen. The couple requested that they would like to hear words of wisdom and advice for their new marriage in order to kiss. A lot of good advice and stories were shared. This option also limited the number of interruptions during dinner because individual people had to go up to the head table and talk on the microphone, all by themselves, in front of everyone (public speaking!!!!)

We also do parent, grandparent and bridal party interviews either before dinner or afterwards, depending on the schedule. We do our utmost to have the majority of these interviews done before dinner to avoid the inevitable inebriation of some of the interviewees, later in the evening. The further an interview is delayed into the evening, the more likely there are going to be some 'loose' speeches. Often the bridal party members and other guests will get on the microphone and tell all sorts of interesting stories about what the couple did when they were in college, or went camping that 'one time', or... These are typically the stories that we will get a call on a few days after the wedding by the bride who will request us to cut out this information, altogether. Or only include it on the couple's final master, and leave it off the parent's videos because most of the time, the parents knew nothing about what happened and should never, ever know. Ever. There are a lot of videos out in the world, produced by "I Do" Productions that have footage missing on the parent copies. Little do they know...

Believe it or not, we have had a number of parents who are about to talk on camera for their kid's wedding video and then right before the camera is turned on asks, "What are we supposed to say?" I usually answer them with, "You know, best wishes, words of wisdom, funny stories about when they were young, something good and embarrassing from their childhood, make something up, whatever. But be sure to keep it 'G' or 'PG' rated because parents and grandparents will be watching." Then the parents say, "Yeah, but what do we say to them? We don't know what to say to them." There have been a few times where I have had to coach the parents on what they should say to their own kids on the video. Awkward, to say the least...

Every so often, I get someone who actually *wants* to get in front of the camera and say something on tape. After their interview, they will hold onto the microphone and start walking around the room interviewing other people as if it were a TV news production. While these people 'interview' the other guests, they act as if they are auditioning for a reality television show; they are hyper and in everybody's face, loud, laughing all the time, etc. A bit annoying, but it gets the job done. The more guests who are on the video, the more interesting the final product is going to be.

Surprise! I'm going to wrap up this chapter with more groomsmen stories. Groomsmen usually do provide the most entertaining interviews on camera. Children can be entertaining, but are sweet more than anything until they decide they are done with their comments and then just drop the microphone on the floor and walk away. Aren't they just adorable?

Anyway, I had one groomsman who had decided to give his interview on camera in the same fashion Jim Carrey, in the movie 'Ace Ventura', spoke to another character; with his derriere. He turned around, back to the camera and then bent over and moved his butt cheeks with his hands as he spoke into the microphone.

Another classic groomsman interview was conducted in a bathroom stall while he sat on the toilet with his pants around his ankles. The interview started with the stall door closed and then it slowly opens to reveal this guy sitting on the toilet reading a newspaper. He looks over the corner of the paper and notices the camera with an, "Oh! Hi! I was just taking care of some business but, since you're here now, I will give you some words of wisdom..." This was the groomsman's idea... We didn't follow him into the bathroom. Like I mentioned earlier, we wait *outside* of the bathroom until they come out and then we pounce.

One groom was from Canada and his three groomsmen decided to pay tribute to him and his country by singing

"I Do"

"O'Canada" while looking over their right shoulder as they stood at the urinals. They said the groom would appreciate it. From an average perspective, the groom has strange friends. Well, maybe the groom is strange, too. To each his own...

Who brought the gun?

Yes, a gun and we're not talking about the security staff hired for the event. Two years ago, at one of my weddings, the band was taking their last break for the evening when the guests started to chatter about hearing popping noises or gun shots. A few people tried looking out the windows but the reflection of the lights on the stage inhibited that effort. A couple of guests, who were leaving at that time, came running back into the reception hall shouting about someone in the parking lot with a gun, and to call the police.

It turned out that one of the groomsmen had a bit too much to drink and had gotten into a fight with his girlfriend. She had left him at the reception and went home early. He was still incredibly angry, went outside, got a gun and just started firing. According to the guests, he wasn't aiming at anything in particular - he was just shooting into the air. Well, the police were called, and he was carted off. I never did ask the couple what had become of that entire incident. Again, that's one of those questions that you'd love to ask but just don't know how to go about it. I'm sure they would rather forget about it as I'm sure that particular groomsman would love to have that memory erased, too.

The other wedding that had guns present, too, would be the family who decided to have fun with the proverbial 'shot gun wedding.' The bride was pregnant, not noticeably, but pregnant. She and her fiancé hadn't spread the impending news to anyone but their families; they wanted to have the wedding first and then make the announcement a few months down the road. Well, as the photography was happening, one of the bride's younger brothers, around 17 years old, though it would be funny to go home and get a few shotguns for the wedding pictures. He arrived back to the church for a surprise, impromptu picture (for the couple) of the groomsmen standing there with smiles and shotguns. Unfortunately, when the picture was being taken in the backyard of the church, guests were starting to arrive. A number of guests had seen the pose, put two and two together, and figured out what was going on.

After the ceremony, people were going through the receiving line giving their best wishes for not only the wedding but also congratulating the couple on the pregnancy and inquiring about the due date. The news spread like wildfire through to the end of the receiving line.

Needless to say, the couple - especially the bride, was very upset and somewhere along the way, the bride's brother got a 'talking to' by his parents. He apologized to his sister and his brother-in-law before entering the reception.

Honeymoon Suites

This is a word of advice for anyone who may have a wedding on the horizon: Give your hotel room key to your Mother. No one, at least in their right mind, will ever open your Mom's purse. That's just not done. Don't fool yourself into thinking the key will be safe by placing it into your coat pocket, or the Bride's purse. Over the course of the reception, these locations are 'fair game.' Either the groom will get hot and take off his coat, leaving the key available for anyone who comes along, or there will be a devious bridesmaid who will pick up the Bride's purse by 'mistake' and take out the key... I'm sure you can see where I'm going with these scenarios. Mom's purse is the safest location for the room key until the couple calls it a night and leaves for their hotel room. I say this because I am now going to tell you about what we have seen over the past 15 years. Of course, the only reason we have seen what we have seen, is because according to the bridal party members, it's more fun to get the honeymoon suite 'decorations' on the video. Here goes...

Depending on how creative (or I should say 'cruel') the bridal party wants to be, one or a number of these 'decorations' have been done to a hotel room:

Vaseline on all the doorknobs

Ice cubes are placed between the sheets

The tub is filled with Jell-O

Plastic wrap across the toilet right underneath the seat

Symmetrical furniture stacking on the bed

The entire room filled with balloons

Ice cream toppings spread between the sheets

Mirrors completely covered by dry soap bars

All the light bulbs are stolen

Blow-up dolls are placed in the bed

The curtains are missing

The bed has been soaked by buckets of ice water

All the luggage is missing

Of course, you could be lucky and have a kind bridal party who will stock your room with champagne, assorted chocolate covered fruits, fresh rose petals, or a basket of 'Wedding Night Goodies', but this is rare. To be on the safe side, just do as I suggest: Give your key to your Mom, and everything will be okay.

Every so often, we will end the video with the groom carrying the bride over the threshold of their suite, and a few times the bride has wound up hitting her head on the door jamb. That always makes for a happy bride! Before the wedding night activities even began, she already had a headache; literally.

Finally, as a wedding videographer, usually we are the last ones to leave the reception site. On one particular evening, I had packed up my equipment and was taking it out to the car via a hotel hallway that had an outside door which was closer to where my car was parked. The closer I got to the end of the hallway, I recognized the person who was sitting on the floor next to the door of a room. The person turned out to be the groom, who was sleeping with a full bucket of ice next to him. I gently woke him up (it took a while) and he told me he couldn't get into his room; he didn't have a key. I left him in the hallway (he was a bit drunk and not going anywhere, anytime soon) and carted my equipment back to the front desk and explained the situation. The front desk tried several attempts at calling his room to tell the bride to open the door and let the groom back into their hotel room. Unfortunately, she had a bit too much to drink too, and was not answering the phone; more than likely sleeping, herself. I next had the front desk call the bride's parents in another room and with the help of the housekeeping staff, the room door was opened and the bride's parents got the groom inside his room. Question: How do you know when you have had too much to drink at your wedding reception? Answer: When your in-laws have to get you into bed and tuck you in! How embarrassing!

Bon Voyage!

For the couple who have their hotel room at a separate location from their reception, a number of them run into the same decoration issues with their cars:

The entire car wrapped in plastic wrap or toilet paper

The car's interior filled with balloons

Vaseline on the door handles or on the stick shift handle

Blow-up dolls in the front seats

Words written with whipped cream, silly string, or shoe polish

Lunch meat slapped onto the car

Condoms used as balloons attached to the car

Lingerie used as flags off the antenna

Ten foot streamers taped to every conceivable surface

Aluminum cans tied to the bumper

Water balloons attached to the wheels

There have also been the couples who have had too much to drink, in which case, I have been known to drive the couple where they need to go, since I'm usually the last person to leave the reception. A wedding videographer's job is never done...

Speaking of driving couples to their hotel do you remember the relatives I mentioned in an earlier chapter? Along with doing the wedding video as a gift, we also hired a limo to take them from their reception to their hotel at the end of the evening, as a surprise. They loaded their luggage and themselves into the limo along with a bunch of their friends and drove around in the middle of the night and went to McDonald's because there was nothing else open, in the area. (You can roll your eyes and start laughing at any time.) When the hour expired, they had the limo drop them back off at the reception hall where they transferred their luggage from the limo into a friends' compact car and squashed themselves in, too, for a ride to their hotel suite. I won't say anything more here; I could, but I won't.

Fifteen Minutes of Fame

In 1992, the KQRS radio station in the Twin Cities started 'The KQ92 Multiple Matrimonies' which was an annual event on their popular morning show. 92 couples were married live on the air, the Friday of each Valentine's Day weekend. 1997 was the final year for this event.

Each year there was a new and interesting cross-section of couples getting married. Each couple received free flowers, a free portrait, a free video of the ceremony (the reception coverage and other options came with a price tag), a free brunch, and a bag of free goodies to take home. The couple had to pay for their marriage license and the formalwear, if desired. The first year's Multiple Matrimonies was held at the Hyatt Regency Downtown in Minneapolis and there were quite a few people there. The following years were held in the East Rotunda of the Mall of America in Bloomington where at least 5,000 people would attend each year.

Each year, we would have to be set up and ready to go by 4:30am. The couples would start arriving at 5:00am

195

when the morning show started. The couples would sign up for their various 'freebies', receive their flowers and get their photography done. Around 8:15am, the 15 minute processional would begin and by 8:30am, the ceremony would commence. From 5:00am to 9:00am, the KQRS Morning Crew would broadcast live providing their listeners with a play-by-play commentary of all the pre-ceremony activities and the entire ceremony. Afterwards, Camp Snoopy would open up for the newly married couples and their guests. At 10:00am, all the couples and their guests would have brunch at one of the restaurants up on the fourth floor followed by a dance. The event would eventually be over by 1:00pm.

Of all the people we ever came into contact with at this event over the years, there is one bride in particular, I remember quite clearly. She was making her way through the line to sign up for the 'freebies' and when she got to me, I asked her to fill in the required information of name, address, etc. so I would know how to contact her once her video was finished. When she was finished filling out the informational sheet, she looked at me and with complete seriousness in her voice asked, "How do you know which couple belongs with which family? Do you have 92 video people here to follow each couple around for the day?" After comprehending that I actually heard someone ask this question and they had actually meant it, I reminded her that she and her fiance were getting married with 91 other couples and that, most likely, they would have these other 91 couples and all of their relatives on their video, too. And no, each couple did not have their own 'video person' for the day. She further said, "Well, there will be people on my video I won't know," to which I replied, "Yes, there will but you are getting your video for free, and that's not a bad price."

Over the years, we have been contacted a few times by the producers of America's Funniest Wedding Videos. We have, with the permissions from couples, submitted footage from different weddings. There is footage from two weddings which stand out, mainly because they were seen by other television show producers who wanted to use the footage, too.

The first would be a couple who was completely covered with Silly String by their bridal party at the reception. They had eight attendants on each side, who at a desgnated time during the toasts, stood up and sprayed the couple with at least 16 cans of Silly String. When all the spraying was done, the couple could not be seen. They were just one huge heap of Silly String. Their footage was shown on America's Funniest Wedding Videos, a show on Weekend London Television in the U.K., and the Maury Povich Show.

The other footage was of a bride being escorted down the aisle by her brother. The brother had been told to say "I do" when asked by the preacher, "Who gives this woman to be married to this man?" As you can imagine, the brother was a bit nervous and wasn't listening very well so, when he and the bride had finished the processional, but before placing her hand into the hand of the groom, the preacher's first question was, "Does anyone here have any objections to this wedding?" for which the brother of the bride blurted out as loud as he could, "I do!" The bride tugged on her brother's arm and said, "Not now!" The congregation burst into uproarious laughter while the brother of the bride was dying of embarrassment. The preacher then leaned over to the brother and whispered, "After this next question, you say 'I do'." The preacher then stood up and proceeded with, "Who gives this woman to be married to this man?" "I do," said the brother who then quietly took his seat.

This video footage was first seen on America's Funniest Wedding Videos and was then picked up by Weekend London Television. After those two shows, The Maury Povich Show called and along with wanting to use the video footage, they also flew the couple out to New York City for the taping of the show, all expenses paid, and a little extra for spending cash. The couple had a great time. My only questions is, where is our all-expenses-paid trip with the extra spending cash? If we hadn't videotaped it, the footage wouldn't exist... Oh, the life of a wedding videographer! Sigh...

June 12, 2004

The last wedding I shot was on June 12, 2004. Actually, that would have been a perfect last shoot for me if one of my assistants hadn't needed to call me to tell me they were three hours away with most of the equipment I needed for my afternoon wedding shoot. WHAT?!?!?!?!?

Turns out, he had picked up an extra bag, by mistake, that morning and left for an out of town wedding. He took one of my cameras, my camera light, all of my camera and light batteries, all of the digital tapes, the microphones, my camera grip, and my sanity. He called me and told me this four hours before my wedding was to begin, a local wedding – only 9 miles away! I couldn't drive a round trip in four hours and his event was scheduled to start in two hours from when he called me so, he couldn't meet me half way. As I have said so often and it seems to hold true, "If I didn't have bad luck, I would have no luck at all!" Why did this have to happen today?!?

I found a cab company that was willing to pick up my equipment and drive it back up to me for $250.00. Actually, that was very 'fare' – they could have really taken advantage of us in that situation. I know it doesn't take $250 to drive 200 miles one-way but, if you weren't planning on driving a 400 mile trip on a sunny Saturday in June (perhaps you had better things to do with your life), I can easily see where it would run $250 for the inconvenience. The cab left our assistant's location exactly three hours before the start time of my wedding. He arrived at my location seven minutes before the bride was to walk down the aisle. Which meant he obeyed the speed limit the entire way! From the cabs I have been in when I've been in Minneapolis, Chicago, and Los Angeles, cabs don't obey the speed limits (generally) so, I thought I would have had at least 30 minutes to finish setting up and look calm. I was pacing around, doing my best to not look suspicious to the bride and groom and their entire family. I have to say, it looked pretty strange to see a cab pull up at a small church in the country. The driver even remarked that this wedding was, "Way out here!"

I had already set up the equipment I did have with me, and for the most part, was ready to go. I just had to set up the back camera, insert tapes in both cameras and wire the groom with the lapel microphone. I had two minutes left to spare; two minutes to lower my blood pressure and stop shaking from the anxiety so I could have a steady picture. After that, the shoot went remarkably smooth, and without any other hitches.

"I Do"

The stress, the anxiety, the realization of knowing that I am the sole person who is ultimately responsible for professionally capturing the entire day's activities and all the memories involved at the very moment they happen is unbelievable. I must be ready at all times for anything to happen; there are no 'Take 2s', no second chances. If I miss the shot, it's gone; absorbed into history. This paragraph best describes 80% of why I need to take a break from this business.

The other 20% would be comprised of some of the couples who have hired "I Do" Productions Wedding Videography, over the years. People who have unrealistic expectations and timelines. People who do not respect and treat others, they have hired for their wedding services, with common and decent courtesy. And there are some people who are just completely unpleasant to everyone with whom they come in contact. Fortunately, I don't remember having too many of these situations but, there have been some 'doosies.' All of those doosies are best left to another book – I will not allow them to exist in this book.

Cheers!

I have heard many toasts and well wishes throughout the years. I will leave you with a few of the memorable ones:

"May you always be blessed with walls for the wind,
A roof for the rain, a warm cup of tea by the fire -
Laughter to cheer you, those you love near you,
And all that your heart may desire."
~ An Olde Gaelic Blessing ~

"May all your troubles be small
and have the pitter patter of little feet."

"May all your 'pains' be champagnes
and all your 'ups and downs' be between
the sheets!"

"I Do"

Maid of Honor (Bride's sister) to Bride:
"I remember, throughout all the years,
you describing the perfect man
whom you would marry:
Sincere, wise, intelligent, funny, caring, gentle,
educated, handsome, well-spoken, etc.
And then you married *this* guy!"

A well spoken, 14 word toast
from my own wedding:
"I hope you'll live each day
as happily as you have lived this one."

I would like to thank you for taking the time out of your busy and hectic life to read about some of my memories from the past 15 years. I hope you have enjoyed them as much as I have enjoyed writing and reliving this 'blast from the past.'

Cheers!!!

Steps Down the Aisle...

This checklist is from the Wedding & Event Directory, a side business I worked on from 1999 to 2003. It has been organized according to order of preparation, but independent of time-frame, since each couple is working under different circumstances. There are many items on this list. You may wish to delegate some of these tasks to family members and your bridal party attendants.

Arrange for both families to meet if not already done

Select a date

Set a budget and determine priorities

Create a 'Personal Wedding Planner' to hold magazine clippings, fabric swatches, contracts, etc.
(e.g. an expandable file folder)

Determine wedding style

Decide on a color scheme

Compile your guest list

"I Do"

Have an engagement portrait taken

Announce engagement in local papers
(w/o exact ceremony locatiom, specific date, and time)

Hire a bridal consultant

Reserve the ceremony and reception sites

Choose one/two people for the responsibility of
'Personal Attendant'

Choose your attendants

Select and order your dress and all accessories

Select and order your attendant's dresses and all
accessories

Choose a caterer, if needed

Arrange for a photographer

Arrange for a videographer

Contact your florist and choose your arrangements

Contact a decorator

Reserve any rental equipment needed
for the ceremony/reception

Select and order favors

Arrange for your reception entertainment

Kiersten Hall

Arrange transportation for yourselves & wedding party

Reserve the musicians and/or soloists for the ceremony

Plan and make reservations for your honeymoon

Order your wedding cake

Select and reserve groom's attire

Select and reserve groomsmen's attire

Select and order your invitations and personalized
stationery, including your thank you notes

Reserve a calligrapher, if needed

Register for gifts

Maintain records of all gifts received
(Send thank you notes immediately upon receipt.)

Purchase wedding rings

Arrange for any necessary transportation
and/or hotel accomodations for out-of-town guests

Help both mothers coordinate and select their apparel

Begin shopping for your trousseau

Experiment with hair style and cut;
take into consideration your veil

"I Do"

Select the location for your rehearsal dinner

Plan ceremony with your officiant

Plan ceremony music with musicians and/or soloists

Purchase gifts for attendants and each other

Purchase guest book, unity candle, toasting goblets, ring pillow, cake knife, and other wedding accessories

Address and mail invitations; include a map and return postage (Invitations should, ideally, be mailed out no less than six weeks before the wedding date.)

Purchase a marriage license

Arrange for final dress fitting for both you and your attendants

Purchase passports and update your immunizations, if your honeymoon is abroad

Make arrangements for hairstylist to be at ceremony site

Make arrangements for manicurist to be at ceremony site

Make arrangements for beautician to be at ceremony site

Call all contracted services to confirm arrangements

Confirm accomodations for guests

Contact any guests who have not responded

Kiersten Hall

Confirm reception seating arrangements

Provide the reception hall/caterer with the total guest count

Confirm ceremony details with your officiant

Confirm all reception details

Schedule the ceremony rehearsal

Invite wedding party and guests to a pre-nuptial/rehearsal dinner

Schedule gift opening party and make any necessary arrangements

Pick up wedding gown and dresses for attendants

Finalize honeymoon plans with your travel agent

Choose responsible attendants for your guest book, gift table, punch bowl

Have ceremony programs printed

Make a timeline of events which will take place on your wedding day. (Distribute this timeline to all services contracted, family members involved, and your bridal party.)

Arrange accomodations for your wedding night

"I Do"

Pick up the wedding rings and make sure they fit properly (Make sure any engraved inscriptions are correct.)

Arrange for professional gown cleaning and preservation

Arrange for floral preservation after the wedding

Pick up men's attire and check for proper fit

Prepare announcements to be mailed on your wedding day or shortly, thereafter

Pack for your honeymoon

Prepare your 'Wedding Day Emergency Kit'*

Break in wedding shoes at home

Write toasts for rehearsal dinner and reception

Purchase a thank you gift for your parents

Arrange to have Post Office hold mail while you are on your honeymoon

Change name (if applicable) on all legal documents

Treat yourself to a day at the spa for a job well done (This is also a nice gift for attendants; most spas offer bridal party packages.)

Get a good night's sleep the night before your wedding day

Remember wedding rings, marriage license, money,
Wedding Day Emergency Kit*, hotel & honeymoon
confirmations on your wedding day

<u>* Wedding Day Emergency Kit *</u>

needle & thread   mints   band-aids & super glue
money for last minute errands
nail polish: your color, your attendant's color
clear polish to fix stocking runs & extra stockings
bags for attendants' clothing
spot remover   anti-static spray   nail file & clippers
feminine products
facial tissues & wet towelettes
make-up & perfume   hair dryer & curling iron
deoderant & talcum powder   lotion
safety pins & plastic bags
mirror, brush, comb, hair spray, bobby pins
waterproof mascara
list of all service providers & their phone numbers

food & drinks:
~ sandwiches, crackers, fruit, etc. to keep up energy levels
~ cooler of clear (stain-avoiding), non-alcoholic drinks

Made in the USA
San Bernardino, CA
12 June 2016